YOU AND YOUR
Border Terrier

David Alderton

THE *Essential* GUIDE

For more than eighteen years, the folk at Veloce have concentrated their publishing efforts on all-things automotive. Now, in a break with tradition, the company launches a new imprint for a new publishing genre!

The Hubble & Hattie imprint – so-called in memory of two, much-loved West Highland Terriers – will be the home of a range of books that cover all things animal, all produced to the same high quality of content and presentation as our motoring books, and offering the same great value for money.

More titles from Hubble & Hattie

www.hubbleandhattie.com

First published in June 2010 by Veloce Publishing Limited, Veloce House, Parkway Farm Business Park, Middle Farm Way, Poundbury, Dorchester, Dorset, DT1 3AR, England.
Fax 01305 250479/e-mail info@veloce.co.uk/web www.veloce.co.uk or www.velocebooks.com.
ISBN: 978-1-845843-19-9 UPC: 6-36847-04319-3
Readers with ideas for books about animals, or animal-related topics, are invited to write to the editorial director of Veloce Publishing at the above address.
British Library Cataloguing in Publication Data – A catalogue record for this book is available from the British Library.
Typesetting, design and page make-up all by Veloce Publishing Ltd on Apple Mac. Printed in India by Replika Press.

Contents

Acknowledgements

Many thanks to Marc Henrie for the majority of the photographic content, and to Ben Stokey and Jude Brooks for the pictures of Milo, courtesy of Mic and Sarah Holmes.

Also to –

Professor S P Dean B Vet Med MRCVS DVR and Mrs Karen Dean; Peter Church with Monty; Hamish, the elderly dog; Hall Place Veterinary Centre, Maidenhead, Berkshire, Helen Heaton of Ryslip Boarding Kennels, and child model, Lily Thomas.

Introduction

Keeping a dog is a serious responsibility, and for any prospective owner there are several issues to be addressed right at the outset. First, do you have the sort of lifestyle that can happily accommodate a dog within it? For example, it is not reasonable or kind to own a dog if you are out at work all day, leaving the dog alone for lengthy periods of time. And can you give a dog the amount of exercise and interaction required to prevent it from becoming obese or bored? Some breeds of dogs, attractive though they may look, are highly active and may become destructive, or even develop other undesirable traits if not exercised regularly. Remember, too, that a young puppy obtained today is likely to be part of your life for a decade or more.

If you are sure you can provide the right kind of physical and emotional environment, however, then your next decision is to decide what kind of dog will be most suitable for your individual circumstances. This is a decision that should never be rushed.

An adaptable companion

Unfortunately, people are frequently drawn to a particular breed largely because of appearance, but this is not the correct basis upon which to determine whether this means it's suitable. It is advisable to delve into the breed's background before buying, so you can discover more about temperament and needs. Luckily, the Border Terrier is an adaptable breed of dog; a fact that is reflected by its enduring popularity. Whether you live on your own or are seeking a family pet, a Border Terrier should develop into a great companion. Border Terriers tend to be more relaxed about life than most other breeds of terrier, and they are also generally quieter.

Equally, however, it is important to appreciate that these terriers will not be suitable for

everyone. One of the most common misapprehensions is that all small dogs are lapdogs; nothing could be further from the truth as far as Border Terriers are concerned. While they are undoubtedly affectionate, they are also naturally active dogs, and certainly not well suited to apartments or other relatively confined dwellings. This is a breed that at the very least needs access to a garden where it can explore, play, and even sunbathe for periods when the weather is suitable. Border Terriers also appreciate longer walks where they can behave in a completely natural manner and show off their personalities to full effect.

Breed background

Anyone who has encountered a Border Terrier will know that although this is a relatively small breed of dog in terms of overall stature, it is one with a big heart. Bold and fearless, these terriers possess a feisty character that belies their size. Indeed, it was the tough, no-nonsense nature of the Border Terrier that was much prized by gamekeepers and others, who employed the dog for all kinds of sporting and hunting activities.

In order to fully appreciate the modern Border Terrier, it is necessary to revisit its original homeland – the once wild border area lying between England and Scotland   to gain an understanding of how the breed developed the qualities that it displays today. The border region is an extensive, mainly upland and mountainous area comprising such places as Dumfries and Galloway in Scotland, and parts of the English counties of Cumbria, County Durham, and Northumberland. Sheep farming has been the predominant occupation there for many centuries, since much of the land is unsuitable for other forms of agriculture.

Predators represented a major threat to the flocks grazed in the borders, particularly at lambing time. While occasional losses to birds of prey sweeping over the moorlands were hard to prevent, regular killing by foxes was something that farmers were more able to control. Hunting offered the best way of trying to combat this, in an era long before the advent of firearms. Special packs of hounds were developed for this purpose, with the aim of pursuing and outrunning their vulpine quarry. There was, however, a major problem. Foxes would retreat to their earths, out of reach of their would-be pursuers. What was required, therefore, was a bold and fearless dog which was small enough to enter the fox's lair and drive it out, or even overpower it underground. It is for this reason that the origins of the word 'terrier' are believed to trace back to the Latin word 'terra' meaning 'earth.'

The precise origins of the Border Terrier have been lost in the mists of time, but it is certain that the breed's ancestors were kept in this region possibly more than 700 years ago. In addition to foxes, they were also pitted against wild cats, which were relatively common then, as well as martens and badgers. The earliest definitive evidence of what are clearly recognizable Border Terriers can be found in a painting by Nathaniel Drake, which was commissioned by William Tufnell Joliffe. The precise date of the portrait is unclear, but it is known that Joliffe kept a pack of hounds until 1765, so it's likely to have been painted earlier. The painting shows Arthur Wentworth, a hunt servant, out on a bitterly cold night accompanied by two terriers trotting alongside the pony he is riding.

Another artist resident in the region was Thomas Bewick, who not only portrayed terriers in some of his engravings, but also provided a description of them in his famous work *History of Quadrupeds*, published in 1790. This confirmed that development of the Border Terrier into the recognizable breed of today had already been largely accomplished by that stage

It was common for wealthy landowners to maintain their own packs of hounds, which often had distinctive patterning. In due course, coloration also became significant as far as terriers were concerned. By the early 1800s, there

A group of Border Terriers with their handler. Bred for work in the countryside, these dogs nevertheless make excellent pets.

Shared ancestry

It is believed that the ancestors of the Bedlington Terrier (bottom), which is often white in colour, as well as the Dandie Dinmont Terrier (whose name commemorates one of Sir Walter Scott's characters), also originated from the same area as the Border Terrier, with all three breeds probably sharing a common ancestry at some point. This is reflected by the fact that, even today, occasional Border Terrier puppies are born with the raised area of soft fur on the centre of the skull which is a feature of both Bedlington Terriers and Dandie Dinmont Terriers. Some suggest that it was crossings between these two terriers that ultimately laid the foundations for the Border Terrier of today.

was a tendency in some quarters to favour black or white terriers, rather than those having reddish coats that could be confused with foxes under certain circumstances. In the Coquet Valley region, within Northumberland's Cheviot Hills, there were three packs of hounds, each associated with terriers. One lineage – the white Redesdale Terrier – died out, in spite of its favoured colouring. However, the coloured Elterwater, or Coquetdale Terrier, which was worked with the Border Foxhounds, survived. The modern Border Terrier lineage is descended from this terrier bloodline, and takes its name from the pack of hounds with which its predecessors were associated.

Establishing the breed

Border Terriers began to appear in the early agricultural shows in the region during the late 1700s, well before dog shows proper began. The famous canine showman Charles Cruft recognized the following that these plucky small dogs enjoyed when he held his first-ever dog show in 1886. He billed the event as the 'First Great Terrier Show,' and it attracted some 600 entries, a significant number of which were Border Terriers. The breed was also subsequently well represented at 'Cruft's Greatest Dog Show,' held in 1891, which marked the start of the modern era of dog shows.

Four years later, there was an initial attempt to form a breed club, but this failed. Then, in 1914, breeders sought to obtain recognition from the Kennel

Recognized by the Kennel Club in 1920, the Border Terrier is frequently seen in the show ring.

Lively and alert, this Border Terrier exemplifies the breed's tough, no-nonsense character.

Unlike many terrier breeds, the Border Terrier is relatively sociable and gets on well with most other dogs. Socialization from an early age is recommended for this reason.

Club for the Border Terrier to be recognized as a breed, but this also came to nothing. Six years later, a subsequent application was granted, but not all Border Terrier owners were thrilled to see their cherished breed being introduced to the show ring. They feared that its working qualities, honed in the Borders region over the course of centuries, would be lost. As a compromise, the Border Terrier Club was hastily set up, its breed standard accepted by the Kennel Club.

Some advocates of the breed responded by setting up the Northumberland Border Terrier Club, calling for a ban on anyone living outside the county being able to breed these terriers. This aim was never realized, however, and the breed's popularity soared as it became known to a much wider dog-loving audience. Fittingly, the first Challenge Certificates were then awarded at a show held in Carlisle, close to the Scottish border. Even today, as a direct legacy of that era, the opening sentence of the Breed Standard dictates that the general appearance of the Border Terrier should be essentially that of a working terrier.

There are still those who worry about the popularity of the Border Terrier and how this could impact on the breed. Unlike many of Britain's other terrier breeds, the Border Terrier is thriving, both in the show ring and as a companion. It typically ranks within the top 20 most popular breeds, based on the Kennel Club's registration figures, and although less numerous in the United States, it still features well within the 100 most popular breeds there. Its rise in popularity has been steady rather than spectacular, suggesting that it is not a breed that will be easily affected by the vagaries of fashion. This may, in part, be a reflection of its appearance, since although the dog is undeniably attractive, it is certainly not cute.

The character of the Border Terrier

It is possible to glean much about the temperament of these dogs from their background. Firstly, although they are relatively small, they are also brave, as befits a breed that was created to venture underground to tackle foxes and do battle with badgers, both of which are formidable adversaries, particularly

Border Terriers will settle well in urban areas, provided they have adequate opportunity to exercise. A park can offer the space they need to explore.

Young Border Terriers investigating an interesting smell. Scenting the ground is an important aspect of this breed's behaviour.

when at bay in the confines of their underground retreats. This means that, in spite of their relatively small size, Border Terriers are not easily intimidated by other dogs that they may encounter – even much larger individuals. This trait can sometimes lead to a potential conflict situation, underlining the importance of your dog being well trained and under control.

Border Terriers are also naturally curious and, particularly when exploring in the countryside, their instincts may lead them to investigate underground burrows. It is important to keep a watchful eye on your pet in case it disappears in such surroundings. The most important thing that must be done to curb the Border Terrier's fearless nature, however, is to train it to return to you when called, which will help keep it out of danger.

On the go

Like most other terriers, the Border Terrier possesses a greater level of energy than its size might suggest. So, if you are seeking a genuine 'lapdog,' do not be fooled into thinking that this breed will meet your requirements. Despite its constant 'on-the-go' attitude, however, the Border Terrier is well suited to a home with older children and teenagers, particularly due to its surprisingly tolerant character. These dogs are also very affectionate and loyal. Border Terriers like to be actively involved in what is happening around them, rather than simply being passive companions. They will also prove to be alert guardians, and once again their vigorous bark rather belies their size. Once they are familiar with a newly arrived visitor, however, they will become quiet – rather than continuing to bark like many other terriers.

Border Terriers are social creatures, and will accept the company of other dogs as well. This pack-oriented aspect of their nature is further reflected by their baying calls, which are rather reminiscent of those of Foxhounds, and could even suggest the involvement of some hound stock in their lineage at some stage in the distant past. You are unlikely to hear this unusual call unless you keep two or more Border Terriers together, but it is very distinctive and quite unlike that of any other terrier.

The hunting instincts of the Border Terrier can occasionally cause it to be aggressive towards cats, but a young puppy reared in a home alongside an established adult cat will soon learn its subordinate position! Again, because of the dog's hunting ancestry, care must obviously be taken if you also keep other potentially vulnerable pets, such as rabbits. However, it is quite possible to teach a Border Terrier to trot alongside a horse, just like its ancestors were accustomed to doing, providing you do this in safe surroundings away from roads.

All-purpose terrier

These terriers are not only responsive to training, but surprisingly adaptable, too, and have performed well in activities including flyball (a competition in which dogs chase balls), and agility, as well as in obedience competitions, and yet they have also been used very successfully as therapy dogs when visiting the sick.

Country dogs at heart, Border Terriers can nevertheless adjust well to suburban living, provided you are willing to ensure your pet receives plenty of exercise every day. Their inclination to dig, however, may sometimes cause friction with other household members who are keen gardeners – particularly as most Border Terriers are always inclined to investigate freshly dug soil. They

Digging and exploring underground is instinctive for young Border Terriers. Because of this, they can easily wriggle under garden fences if there's a gap.

are also adept at tunnelling, and are able to turn even a small gap under a fence into an escape route from your garden, a behaviour especially prevalent in dogs that become bored.

Defining the standard

The official standard provides a written description of the characteristic

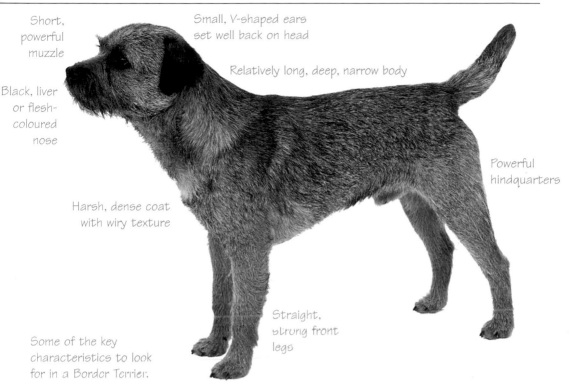

Short, powerful muzzle

Small, V-shaped ears set well back on head

Relatively long, deep, narrow body

Black, liver or flesh-coloured nose

Powerful hindquarters

Harsh, dense coat with wiry texture

Straight, strong front legs

Some of the key characteristics to look for in a Border Terrier.

features of a particular breed, with that of the Border Terrier having remained essentially unaltered to any significant extent for over 90 years.

HEAD

The Border Terrier's distinctive appearance stems partly from the otter-like shape of its head. The muzzle is short and powerful, and the skull relatively broad. The ears should be quite small and V shaped, hanging forwards down over the cheeks. The bite – which refers to the way that the jaws meet – should be a scissor bite, meaning that the upper teeth overlap those in the lower jaw when the mouth is closed; however, a level bite, in which the upper and lower teeth meet evenly, is also acceptable. The canine teeth located at each corner of the mouth are relatively large, as is common in terriers.

BODY

Working back along the body, the neck is powerful, with the body being deep, as well as narrow and quite long. This provides for good lung capacity, without hindering the movement of the terrier when it is underground. Power is evident in the loins, linking with the so called 'racy' hindquarters, which traditionally enabled these terriers to trot long distances during a day's work alongside a horse.

LEGS

The Border Terrier's front legs should be straight, and the paws quite small, although the pads are thick, affording good protection against injury. This attribute does, however, mean that the nails tend not to wear down, particularly if the terrier is not walking on hard surfaces such as pavements, and so may need to be regularly trimmed back.

TAIL

The tail is relatively short and tapers along its length, and is positioned or 'set' quite high on the back. It can be carried upright when the terrier is alert, but does not curl forward over the back at all.

COAT

The coat is quite distinctive. It has a harsh, wiry texture and is dense, with an undercoat that lies close to the skin. This is also thick, providing additional protection from injury in the case of working terriers. The coat is ideally suited to a breed that traditionally worked outdoors in all weathers. The double layering means that it is water-resistant, helping to protect against rain and snow, and also does not get dirty easily.

This wheaten Border Terrier shows the relatively short tail positioned high on the back, and tapering along its length.

COLOURS

There are four different colours: wheaten; red; grizzle and tan; or blue and tan, but only the last two are common. Interestingly, the coat of the latter variety frequently seems to be harsher, with correspondingly easier care Colouring is not considered a particular feature of the breed, however, and breeders do not usually breed for this characteristic.

Young Border Terrier

puppies may have odd, white patches on their toes, and this characteristic is regarded as a show fault, although they may often disappear with age. In addition, some individuals can have a small patch of white on the chest, but this is not penalized for show purposes. Equally, the nose is normally black in colour, but may sometimes be liver or occasionally flesh-coloured. The eyes, however, are always dark in appearance.

This grizzle-and-tan Border Terrier has a small area of white on the chest. However, this is not considered a fault in the breed.

SIZE

Male Border Terriers may grow slightly larger than bitches. Adult males typically weigh 13-15lb (5.9-7.1kg), whereas adult females weigh 11.5-14lb (5.1-6.4kg). It is, of course, quite possible for a Border Terrier of either sex to weigh more, but this is likely to indicate that the individual is overweight, and action needs to be taken without delay to slim down the dog before its health is adversely affected. There is no height specified for Border Terriers, but they average between 11 and 13in (28-33cm), when measured in traditional style to the withers, which is the point marking the top of the shoulder.

Health matters

Studies carried out by the Kennel Club involving all registered breeds have confirmed the overall health and vitality of the Border Terrier. The breed's typical lifespan of 14 years is longer than average, and these terriers generally have few health problems. In fact, the major cause of death in the survey was as a result of old age. In terms of health problems which were highlighted, the most significant related to disorders affecting the reproductive tract, particularly of bitches. Pet owners can significantly reduce the risk of such problems occurring by neutering, which is highly recommended in any event (see page 83).

A thorough health check is important for puppies, and an annual check-up for seemingly healthy older dogs is recommended, too.

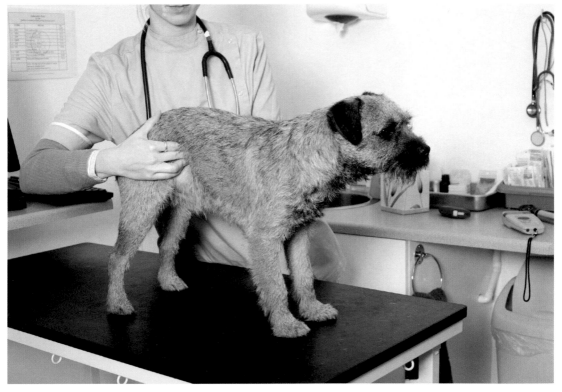

Part of the reason why the Border Terrier has remained such a healthy breed probably stems from its judging standard. This was based on its working ancestor, which has meant that appearance has changed relatively little over the course of almost a century. In common with other breeds, however, certain inherited health problems are recognized.

One very widespread disease, which also affects many other breeds, is hip

An ocular examination in progress. Like many breeds, Border Terriers can be susceptible to the eye condition known as progressive retinal atrophy (PRA).

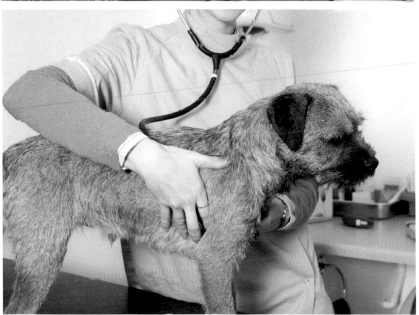

Listening to the heart with a stethoscope. Heart defects are not unknown in the breed.

dysplasia; only Greyhounds are known to be free from this condition. Signs of this ailment, such as a persistent limp, are not typically seen in puppies, but appear in young adult dogs. The problem results from the cup-shaped acetabulum on the pelvis being too shallow to accommodate the rounded head of the upper leg bone, known as the femur, which causes the joint to be unstable. Although there is no real corrective treatment for the condition, it is possible for breeding stock over a year old to be scored for hip dysplasia following an X-ray examination, with only those getting a low score being used for breeding purposes.

Another widespread inherited ailment afflicting not just Border Terrier bloodlines but also many other breeds is progressive retinal atrophy (PRA). This condition develops in young or middle-aged adults, and affects the retina at the back of each eye, where the image is formed. The first signs are likely to become evident in a dark room, with an affected individual walking into objects. PRA will worsen over time, as its name suggests, leading to total blindness. Once again, there is unfortunately no treatment, but a screening programme means that it should be possible to eliminate the problem from breeding lines. As with hip dysplasia, check that the parents of any puppy you are thinking of acquiring have been checked for this condition.

A more specific, although uncommon, inherited problem in Border Terriers is a congenital ventricular septal defect, resulting in what is commonly known as a 'hole in the heart.' This condition manifests itself in the internal partition, or septum, separating the right and left ventricles of the heart. A vet should be able to hear the resulting murmur, caused by turbulence in the blood flow, when listening to a puppy's heart. Further examination to confirm and evaluate the condition may entail the use of an echocardiogram once a puppy is about four months old. This is because the detection of a murmur is not necessarily diagnostic, and may have other causes. In mild cases, the gap in the septal wall may close spontaneously with age, but such dogs must not be used for breeding purposes, since they will still be carrying the defective genes.

Other congenital conditions may crop up occasionally, but if you find a reputable breeder, the likelihood is that your puppy will be free of such problems. An initial veterinary check can also do much to ease any worries you may have in this regard, and should also provide a safeguard. Breeders have a responsibility to ensure that their puppies are healthy when they sell them.

Ownership costs

As well as the cost of purchasing a puppy, it is important not to overlook the other initial expenditure involved. These can include veterinary costs, official breed registration, the purchase of feeding bowls and other equipment such as a collar and lead, toys, a bed, and food, of course. You may also need to spend money ensuring that your garden is securely fenced, as well as preventing your puppy from escaping under a gate. Almost inevitably there will be some

'accidents,' as well as some damage around the home – particularly when the puppy is teething, at around six months of age. If you are alert to your pet's needs, however, and spend plenty of time with the young terrier, these associated costs can be kept to a minimum.

Being relatively small dogs, Border Terriers are not expensive to feed. As a guide, they will need about one and a half standard 14oz (400g) cans of complete food per day, three to four pouches of the 5oz (150g) size, or the same weight and number of home-cooked meals. Being generally healthy and hardy animals, the veterinary costs for a Border Terrier should be minimal,

Grooming a Border Terrier to keep its coat clean is not time-consuming, although periodic professional grooming will maintain the coat in the best condition.

aside from the routine costs of vaccinations and parasite treatments. Although these will be influenced to some extent by where you live, both represent a relatively minor expense. It may be worth taking out pet insurance (see page 32), in case your terrier suffers, or causes, an accident; note, however, that the cost of cover usually rises significantly with age. The cost of neutering – a worthwhile procedure – will not be covered by insurance. This operation is cheaper to perform on a male dog, and is usually carried out from six months of age onwards. Bitches are normally spayed slightly later, after their first season.

Professional grooming is an on-going expense that you will need to meet if you want your pet to look its best. It is possible to clip the coat easily at home, but this affects its structure, causing it to lose its distinctive texture and making it softer. As an alternative, Border Terriers can be hand-stripped twice a year to maintain their coat in the best possible condition. This is something that can be arranged through a grooming salon, with the cost depending partly on where you live.

You also need to bear in mind the cost of providing kennelling or some other suitable arrangement for your Border Terrier when you go on holiday. However, since the Border Terrier is a relatively small breed you are likely to be charged less at such establishments than if, for example, you had a Great Dane. It may sometimes be possible to take your pet with you on holiday, but bear in mind when staying in hotels or similar accommodation that there is often a charge for allowing dogs to accompany you. You may also be able to take your pet abroad. Owners living in the UK, for example, can travel with their dogs to mainland Europe and some other countries, providing they follow the requirements of the so-called Pet Passport Scheme (see page 84), although there are some veterinary costs involved in sorting out the paperwork. This may still work out cheaper than arranging for your pet to stay in a boarding kennel, and, of course, be far nicer than leaving your companion behind!

Choosing & buying

Once you have decided that you would like a Border Terrier, there are some critical decisions to be made right at the outset. The most important, initially, will be to decide on the age and gender of your new pet. Many people prefer to have a puppy, and this can be a very desirable option for several reasons. First of all, you will know the age of the terrier with certainty. Perhaps more significantly, there is a unique opportunity to form a very close bond with your companion, in a way that is much harder to achieve with an older dog.

Nevertheless, an older Border Terrier can offer certain advantages over a puppy, assuming you can be sure of its background. You probably won't need to house-train an older dog (unless it has always lived in kennels), but you are likely to have to work harder at first to win its confidence. In this respect, a

Which will you choose – an older dog or a puppy? Both make delightful companions, but your decision will be influenced partly by individual circumstances.

Dog or bitch?

The choice of gender is not necessarily significant, although if you are particularly interested in showing your dog, a young bitch (female) may be a better choice, since you then have the possibility of developing your own bloodline. Some owners also feel that bitches can be more affectionate than dogs (males), although this is certainly not a universal view. If you are seeking two puppies, then choosing bitches is possibly a better option, although siblings of either sex will usually get along together without any problems.

There are also some drawbacks with female dogs because of the regular reproductive periods – called 'seasons' – which they undergo twice a year. If you are not intending to keep your terrier for breeding purposes, it is recommended that you arrange for your pet to be neutered. This surgery is more costly and potentially riskier for a bitch than for a male dog, however, because the surgery involved is more invasive.

Another decision will involve the gender of your puppy. An early veterinary check soon after purchase is essential.

full-grown Border Terrier is a good choice for people living on their own, or at least for those without children about, who may have more time to devote to their new companion. It is not usually advisable to introduce an adult dog to a home where younger children are present, in any case. Puppies are more tolerant and adaptable, and will settle in to new surroundings more quickly, and will more readily accept their place at the bottom of the family 'pecking order.'

When to buy

Late spring is the best time of year to start with a young puppy. This gives you the opportunity to use the summer months to train your new dog, when the days are longer and the weather is likely to be better – although as far as Border Terriers are concerned, this is not necessarily a major consideration, since they are happy outdoors in all weathers. The key is to choose a suitable time when you will be around to accustom your pet to its new surroundings. Never feel pressured to take a young puppy if you are about to go away on holiday within a few weeks of acquiring your new pet. This is exactly when you need to be establishing a bond with the puppy, and having to put the young terrier into kennels at this stage will interfere with the process. The same applies in the case of an adult dog.

It is not usually recommended to acquire a young puppy at Christmas, simply because most family homes are more chaotic at this time of year than at other times. With people being busy, there is also less opportunity to focus on the terrier's needs, and a bored puppy is likely to become destructive. Nevertheless, if you are on your own and are anticipating a quiet festive break, then this gives the option to settle your new pet into your home without any major distractions – it depends very much on your individual circumstances. The choice of when to obtain a puppy may be influenced by other factors over which you have no control. For example, puppies tend to be more readily available at certain times of the year – linked to the breeding cycles – whereas an older dog can potentially be available at any time.

When you buy from a reputable breeder, you should have the opportunity of seeing youngsters interacting with at least one of their parents, helping you to gain an insight to your prospective dog's background.

Obtaining a Border Terrier

There are two main sources for obtaining your new dog. The first option is to buy from a breeder. You can find reputable breeders by contacting the Kennel Club in the area where you live; it usually has a list, or can put you in touch with breed clubs. There's no guarantee that there will be puppies available when you contact them, however; you may need to be patient, especially if you have set your heart on a particular colour. Alternatively, you can take a more direct approach by visiting dog shows and talking with breeders to discover who may have litters for sale in the foreseeable future.

If you are purchasing a Border Terrier from an established exhibition lineage, this will be reflected in the asking price. The cost of the puppy will be influenced by both the dog's pedigree and the breeder's assessment of its potential in the show ring. The fact that a breeder may part with a puppy which displays a fault does not mean that the puppy is unhealthy, as all reputable breeders will screen their breeding stock for detectable inherited ailments. 'Faults' in this case should refer to the breed's judging standard. These should be minor variants that do not affect the physical ability of the puppy in any way. It may be, for example, that its ears are too large, or that there are conspicuous white patches on its feet. Such a dog may never become a champion, but will still develop into a delightful companion. Puppies will be ready to go to a new home from about eight weeks on. However, if you are set on having a potential show dog, it will be better to seek out an older animal – one at least six months

All Border Terrier puppies are appealing! It can be very hard to decide on a particular puppy, particularly if you are seeking an individual that will be both pet and show dog.

old, because even experienced breeders may find it difficult to pick out at a young age a Border Terrier that is likely to do well in the show ring later in life. The dog can change significantly as it grows older, with its bite, for example, being particularly inconsistent in the early stages. It may be that you are more interested in having a Border Terrier as a working companion, in which case, it will be better to find a breeder whose dogs excel in this regard.

Another aspect to consider is how far you are willing to travel in search of a puppy. If you are seeking a Border Terrier simply as a pet, you may be able to obtain one locally from a home breeder rather than from an exhibitor, but you need to be certain that the dog is genuinely home-bred and does not come from a puppy farm. Puppy farms have a bad reputation because the welfare of the dogs is often seriously compromised in the pursuit of profit. Puppies reared in the home are likely to be already well socialized towards people, whereas if they have been brought up in a kennel and had little human contact – which is usually the case on puppy farms – they will be shy and withdrawn, making it much harder to win their confidence.

If you see an advertisement for Border Terrier puppies in a local newspaper or on the internet, first check whether you can see both parents, or at least the

An older dog that has established habits and ways may take longer to settle in a new home.

Puppies whose parents have excelled in the show ring are themselves more likely to do well in this environment.

mother (dam), with the puppies. The dam should appear relaxed, and be in good condition; a good indication that the puppies are genuinely home-bred. The other very important consideration is to check that both parents were screened for inherited ailments. The sad fact is that, although you might be able to buy a puppy cheaper from a home breeder rather than an exhibitor, you could subsequently end up spending much more on your new pet in terms of health care if it develops a condition such as hip dysplasia.

Mature individuals

Older Border Terriers sometimes find themselves in search of new homes through rescue organizations. There can be a variety of reasons for this – for example, it may be that the terrier's previous owner has died, or that the family is emigrating and cannot take their pet with them. Do not be surprised to find yourself being questioned carefully if you want to take a Border Terrier from a rescue organization. Before allowing you to take the dog, it will almost certainly want to visit you first to check that you can provide a suitable, permanent home.

It is quite possible that, if you acquire an adult Border Terrier, it may already be fairly well trained.

It is equally important for you to try and discover as much as possible about the terrier's background under these circumstances. Unfortunately, people do not always give an honest account of why they need to find a new home for their pet when handing it in at a rescue centre. Sometimes it can be because the dog has a behavioural problem, and such animals may not be suitable for a home with young children or other pets, such as cats. The situation will be more complicated if the Border Terrier has been abandoned, since virtually nothing may be known about its past. However, with patience and

It is always a good idea to try to see a litter early – if only to have the pick of available puppies!

love, it is usually possible to win the confidence of these animals, even if they have been mistreated. Furthermore, if you take on an abandoned Border Terrier, the rescue organization concerned will also usually provide assistance should an unforeseen problem become apparent when your new pet is settling in with you, and this can be reassuring.

Breeders are also sometimes willing to home older dogs, perhaps once their show careers have come to an end. Such individuals often settle better than dogs that have been rescued, simply because they have been well trained and come from a more stable background. Nevertheless, a period of adjustment will be required, and you will need to be patient – it *is* actually possible to teach an old dog new tricks, but it does take longer than with a puppy!

Choosing a puppy

If possible, arrange to see the litter of puppies before they are independent, as you can then decide if one of them appeals to you. Even so, do not feel

You may well find that one of the puppies chooses you!

The breed's inquisitive, playful nature is apparent from a very early age.

under pressure to buy the first one that you are offered. As with any other long-term relationship, this decision should not be rushed. If you are unsure for any reason, or want to look elsewhere, then do so. Most breeders will understand this, particularly if you make it clear that you are serious about obtaining a Border Terrier. If you decide on a puppy that is not yet ready to leave its mother, however, the breeder will probably expect a deposit to reserve it for you.

Checking the puppy's health

Young puppies may be unsteady on their feet, but you can still gain insights to other aspects of their state of health. When picking up the puppy, you should not be able to feel any marked swelling in the umbilical area (the mid-line on the puppy's tummy), since this could be indicative of a hernia, a condition which may need corrective surgery later in life. Look for any signs of parasites, although these will not usually be evident if the breeder is reputable. When holding the puppy, inspect its coat by brushing the coat against the way it lies: tiny egg cases of lice stick to individual hairs, whereas dark specks in the coat will indicate flea dirt. Look at the puppy's profile, too; a particularly pot-bellied appearance is often indicative of intestinal worms. Check inside the ears as well. These should be clean, with none of the build-up of wax that can be linked to the presence of ear mites. Likewise check for discharge from the pup's eyes and nose, and that there are no signs of diarrhoea.

Do not worry too much about other aspects of the puppy's health. The

Arranging for a puppy to stand in the breed's classic show pose gives the best opportunity of assessing its show potential.

Check the puppy's ears thoroughly to make sure they are clean.

Another important feature to check is the bite – the way in which the jaws meet (see page 27). A Border Terrier should have a scissor bite, with the upper teeth just overlapping the front teeth in the lower jaw, although a level bite is acceptable. Check the general condition of the teeth at the same time.

Check the coat for any sign of parasites. You may have to look closely to spot any lice egg cases, which will be 'glued' to individual hairs.

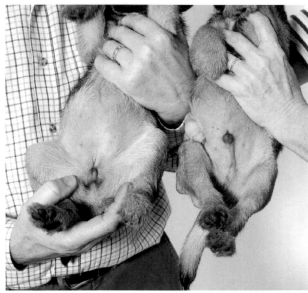

Above right: A young bitch or female puppy (left) and a young dog or male puppy. The dog's testes will not have descended into the scrotum at this early age.

pup will need to be checked out by your vet and, if any major problem is found at this stage, such as a heart condition, this can be taken up with the breeder. Consumer protection laws will afford you protection if the puppy is ill at the time it is sold to you, although obviously you will rapidly form an attachment to your new pet and may not want to return it to the breeder. The advice of an experienced vet will be vital under these circumstances.

Choosing an older dog

In addition to discovering as much as possible about its background, it is advisable to take the Border Terrier you are thinking of homing for several walks, if possible, before you reach a final decision. This will give you some idea of how the dog reacts to you, and will also provide you with some indication of its general behaviour, including how well it responds to basic instructions and walking on the lead. Unless the dog can be let free in an enclosed run, you probably won't be able to judge how it behaves off the lead at this stage, however.

Pet insurance

Veterinary costs have risen steeply in recent years, and although these reflect the advances in veterinary care that have occurred, it may pay you to insure your new pet. A wide variety of policies are now available, and it is important

Buying a puppy checklist

✓ Locate breeders
✓ Arrange to visit by appointment
✓ Carry out basic physical check
✓ Decide if you want to place a deposit on a
  puppy. If so, obtain a receipt
✓ Arrange to collect the puppy once it is
  fully weaned
✓ Check it over again at this stage, and
  pay the balance, assuming all is well
✓ Obtain a diet sheet, showing what the
  puppy is eating, so you can prepare
  for its arrival
✓ Ask for a signed vaccination certificate
  and deworming information at the time
  of collection
✓ If available, take pedigree papers and
  notify change of ownership to
  registration body

Buying an older dog checklist

✓ Contact rescue centres/breeders
✓ Arrange to visit by appointment
✓ Interact with the dog, as permitted
  by the staff
✓ Be prepared to have a home visit
✓ Pick up the terrier, along with
  vaccination certificate, and pay a
  re-homing fee
✓ Keep in touch with the centre,
  alerting it to any problems
  you encounter

Young Border Terriers need to be trained to walk on a lead, and can only be taken out into public areas after their vaccinations are complete.

to check the terms carefully, to be certain that you are only buying the appropriate cover for your individual circumstances. In addition to covering veterinary costs, pet insurance policies usually offer extra protection in case of holiday cancellation if your pet is ill or strays, together with help towards the cost of producing 'lost' posters in the latter event.

The propensity of Border Terrier puppies for chewing, particularly during their teething phase, means that they can easily swallow harmful objects, and this can sometimes necessitate surgery. Cover for this type of emergency care can be very important, therefore, especially in the case of younger dogs. Damage caused around the home by your pet is not covered by a veterinary insurance policy, however. This is something that would need to be claimed under a household policy, so check that your existing cover allows you to claim for such accidental damage. Routine veterinary costs for vaccines and deworming are also excluded under pet health policies.

Above right: Persuading your puppy to concentrate on what is required is a very important lesson.

Even though puppies and young dogs are far less likely to fall seriously ill than older individuals, they are particularly susceptible to accidents. Border Terriers in general, and puppies in particular, have no road sense, and are at serious risk if they escape from their home surroundings. Perhaps the most important aspect of insurance cover, as far as dogs are concerned, is third party liability. Under the law, if your dog runs out into the road and causes an accident or bites someone, you can potentially be held liable as its owner. Since awards of damages under these circumstances can sometimes be very large, depending on the resulting injuries, it is vital to have adequate cover. This may already be included under an existing household policy, although equally, it may be featured as part of a pet insurance scheme, but always check to see that you are covered should the worst happen.

Preparing for your new pet

There is a range of equipment that you will need to buy for your Border Terrier, in advance of its arrival. Food and water bowls are essential. Stainless steel bowls are tough, but can be tipped over rather easily. Because of their shape, lightweight plastic bowls are not easily tipped over, and they have the advantage of being easy to clean. However, your pet may chew them, so be prepared to buy replacements. Traditional ceramic containers are both easy to clean and chew-proof, although they will readily break if dropped. A feeding mat on which you can stand the bowls may also be useful, helping to prevent any spillage on to the floor. This simply needs to be wiped over regularly.

A collar, lead and harness are necessary, although you will not be able to take a young puppy out until after it has finished its course of vaccinations at three months old. Nevertheless, it's a good idea to accustom a young Border Terrier to wearing a collar at an early age. You must buy a collar of the right size, and let it out or replace it as your puppy grows, so that it does not become too tight. As a guide, in order to be a comfortable fit, you must be able to slide two fingers side by side between the collar and the puppy's neck. Traditional leather collars are softer on the skin than nylon ones, but are not necessarily so easy to clean if your terrier has ventured underground and become muddy. As an alternative, there are now collars made from materials like hemp canvas, for example, which are machine-washable and are quite soft on the skin and coat. An older dog may already have a collar and lead when you acquire it. You should also get a name disc to fit to the collar, which incorporates your home address and (preferably) your mobile phone number. If your pet strays at any stage, it will be easy for someone finding your pet to contact you straightaway. Microchipping can also help to get you reunited with a lost pet (see page 52). There are various sorts of leads available, including extending ones which allow your dog more freedom. Whatever type of lead you buy, make sure it is an appropriate thickness and length.

It is probably not worthwhile purchasing a bed for your puppy until it has finished teething, around six months of age, since it's quite likely to be destroyed by being chewed. A cut down cardboard box, lined with old newspaper and a cushion or soft blanket is a good idea, and can easily be replaced if necessary. For older dogs, there are many choices of a bed, ranging from traditional wicker lined with a large cushion or blanket, through to a beanbag that will allow the terrier to stretch out. A good alternative to these is a single duvet folded in half,

Basic equipment available for your new pet will include a food bowl (top right) and drinking bowl, plus various types and sizes of collars and leads.

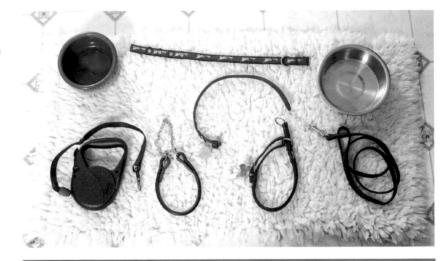

Plastic beds are useful for older Border Terriers, but a bed of this type is a tempting object for a puppy to chew when it is teething.

Terriers are great escapologists, so before your pet arrives be sure to check that your garden is safe and secure. Walk carefully around the entire perimeter, looking for any gaps under the fence or under gates that could allow your dog to start digging and get out, or simply slip out from underneath. You should also keep looking for any signs that your dog is trying to burrow out at any stage, which is most likely to happen if it is left alone for long periods.

There are also potential dangers within the home, particularly from trailing electrical cables that are likely to be chewed by a puppy, especially when it is teething. These need to be placed out of reach as far as possible, with electrical equipment unplugged when not in use. In order to keep your puppy safe at home, there will be times when you need to confine it – so that it cannot run out into the street, for example, when the front door is open. There are wire pens, sometimes called crates, which you can use for this purpose. It is a good idea to put your puppy in one of these when you go out, so it cannot come to any harm. Note, though, that these should not be used to confine your puppy other than when strictly necessary, as it is not kind to leave an animal restrained in this way for long periods or on a regular basis.

Check for gaps under your fence, and fix these to prevent your puppy slipping out here.

encased in homemade covers that can be easily changed and washed. They often seem to prefer this latter type of sleeping arrangement, particularly if it is located close to a radiator.

Bringing your new pet home

A crate as described previously can be used as a travelling pen in the car. This avoids the need to have a separate dog guard, whilst ensuring that your dog can travel safely and securely in the back of your car. These units can be collapsed flat when not in use.

When you first bring your puppy home, however, it may be better to carry it in a secure plastic corrugated carrier, lined with old newspaper. On top of this, place an old towel which has its dam's scent. Her familiar smell will reassure the puppy when it is on its own for the first time, and can help it settle. Position the carrier on the floor behind one of the front seats, where it will be secure throughout the duration of the journey. Rubber floor mats will also prevent any seepage of urine out of the container from getting on to the

Travelling crates are the easiest and safest means of transporting your pet in a car. It is advisable to put a liner beneath the crate, in case of any accidents. As an alternative to a crate, you could use a dog guard.

carpets or upholstery of the car. It is possible that your puppy may become car sick, particularly if you have a long journey to cover, but this is not a serious cause for concern. Puppies usually soon learn to travel without any problem.

Should you be relying on public transport, use an enclosed container in which to carry home your puppy. It is especially important that you do not set your puppy down or allow it to walk in public places at this stage, since it will not be fully protected against serious infectious diseases until it has completed its initial course of vaccinations (see page 54). You can bring back an adult Border Terrier on a leash, but be aware that not only will your new pet be in strange surroundings, it will also not know you well, and may be more nervous than normal as a result. Be sure to keep your new pet away from other dogs in case it reacts aggressively at this stage.

Even if you are acquiring an older dog, it is important to place it in a suitable crate to stop it jumping around in your vehicle. Although there are seat belts that dogs can wear to restrain them in a vehicle, their use is not recommended at the outset unless your dog is used to them. They could cause serious distress, and might even result in damage to the seat as the terrier struggles in an attempt to free itself.

Warning!

Always remember that if you break your journey home, you should never, ever leave your new companion in the vehicle on its own. Even on only a moderately warm day, the temperature in the interior can potentially rise to a fatal level within minutes.

Oppposite: Some dogs settle better in covered crates. Always be certain the door is properly closed before lifting the crate.

Settling in

If possible, aim to collect your new pet early in the day so that it has plenty of time to explore and settle into its new surroundings before night-time (this should help to ensure that you have a more peaceful night's sleep as well!) Remember, it is quite usual for a puppy to feel distressed after being separated from its mother and littermates, even though it is fully weaned. Try to keep the young terrier awake until you are ready for bed, and then leave it in its crate, complete with a bed that includes the towel with its mother's scent.

Always support a puppy's hindquarters securely when lifting it, and wear long sleeves to avoid being scratched by its claws.

Having a place where
you can confine
a young puppy at
times is strongly
recommended. This
cage can later be
used as a carrying
container in your
car.

Sleeping arrangements

Don't be surprised if you are woken by crying at some stage in the night. Hard though it may be to do, the best thing, if possible, is to ignore this: if you go down and try to reassure your new pet, you are likely to establish a precedent, as your puppy will quickly realise that crying will guarantee your attention. Worse will follow if you take the puppy into your bedroom, even assuming you have a plastic tray on which the crate can rest, as the puppy may simply continue crying in the bedroom, making it even harder for you to sleep …

An adult Border Terrier should be exercised last thing at night and then, hopefully, it will be tired and ready to go to sleep. Try to encourage it to sleep in the bed that you have provided, but do not be surprised if, especially at first, the animal insists on sleeping elsewhere. It can be difficult to decide which part of the house is most suitable for this purpose: the kitchen is, perhaps, an obvious place, partly because the floor covering (probably tiles or cushion flooring) will be easier to clean than carpet in the even of an accident. During the daytime, however, the kitchen often tends to be a fairly busy thoroughfare and is potentially dangerous, especially with hot pans and boiling water being moved on and off the stove. A major advantage of using the kitchen, however, is that it is usually has access to the outside, which can be useful when house-training a puppy. It will then be a matter of keeping your pet confined in its

Always walk your dog on the side farthest from the road, so that it cannot step out into danger.

crate when you are cooking, to ensure that there is no risk of a potentially serious accident.

House rules

While it is advisable to restrict a young puppy to a few rooms until it is fully house-trained, an older, house-trained Border Terrier can be allowed to wander more freely through the home. But start as you mean to go on: if, for example, you don't want your new pet to sleep on armchairs and sofas, do not encourage this behaviour at the outset and then expect the terrier to realize later that this is no longer acceptable. It is also important to encourage an adult

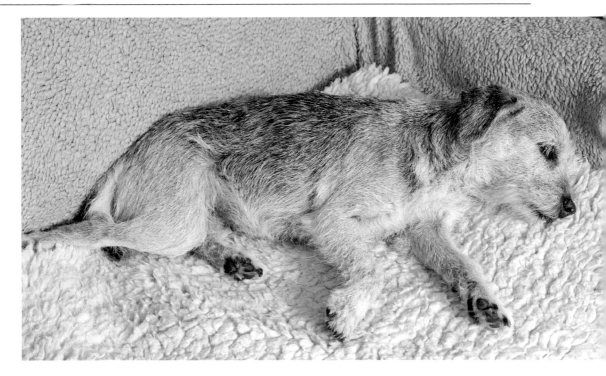

dog into the garden to relieve itself regularly. Aim to develop a routine, so that – particularly first thing in the morning, and then last thing at night – your terrier is allowed out for this purpose – although it will also need to go out during the day, too, of course. You should also establish, and reinforce (firmly but kindly), any rules you wish to set regarding whether or not the dog is allowed upstairs. A guard fixed at the bottom of the stairs will help train a dog to remain at ground level. Similarly, it is important to ensure your dog doesn't get into the habit of sitting in the front seat of your car; you can buy a guard that will safely retain the animal in the boot area of a hatchback or estate car, you can use the crate method described on pages 37/38, or, using a special harness designed for dogs, strap the dog to the seat via the car's seat belt.

It is important to start reinforcing training from the outset, so that bad habits do not develop. Your dog may have an inclination to bark repeatedly if left outside on its own for long periods, for example, which can prove particularly annoying to the neighbours. Call the dog inside after a relatively short time, therefore, before it starts to become bored and begins to bark. Even if the dog doesn't make a noise, it may begin to investigate the possibility of wandering further afield if left unattended outside for too long. Be particularly careful

If you allow your puppy on the furniture, you may want to place a cover on first to protect it.

If left alone, puppies are likely to find ways to amuse themselves out of sight, which can lead to problems ...

when leaving an adult Border Terrier alone in the home for the first time, particularly if you do not know its background, since it may be destructive; best to confine it to a single room as a damage limitation exercise. If possible, always exercise your pet before you go out, and, with any luck, it should then sleep, rather than look for something to relieve its boredom. Furthermore, try to keep your absences as short as possible at first. Be particularly wary about leaving the terrier confined in the kitchen: during its explorations it may inadvertently turn on the gas or electricity on the cooker with its paws.

Other pets

Never leave a newly-acquired Border Terrier – especially an adult dog – alone in a room with a cat, as this could lead to bloodshed. Allow the cat and the dog to meet on neutral territory (such as the garden) if possible, and make sure you are also present. At first, the cat is likely to ignore the dog – although it will probably regard it somewhat warily. If the terrier starts to make a nuisance of itself, however, the cat is likely to run off, and will almost inevitably be pursued by the dog. Step in at once to prevent the risk of any injury. If the cat is cornered it will lash out but, given the Border Terrier's bravery, this is not

Out in the garden,
your puppy is
likely to encounter
neighbourhood cats,
even if you do not
have a cat of your
own.

usually sufficient to deter the dog from pressing home its attack. After all, the ancestors of these terriers were pitched against the much more ferocious native wildcat when these felids were once widespread in Britain.

If you have chosen a puppy rather than an adult dog, you should find it easier to establish domestic harmony between dog and cat. At first, the cat is likely to be rather withdrawn in the company of the terrier, walking warily around the newcomer, and perhaps not venturing indoors as much as usual. Be prepared to deal with any signs of over-exuberance on the part of the dog that could spill over into aggression. Keep a water pistol to hand, so that if the young terrier starts to threaten the cat, you can distract the dog by aiming a small jet of water at it, at the same time giving the firm command 'No.' You may need to repeat this action on a number of occasions until the dog learns to modify its behaviour. The cat may try to defend itself under these circumstances, not only by hissing menacingly, but also by lashing out at the puppy with its claws. It is equally important to ensure that the puppy doesn't become badly scratched by the cat during these encounters.

Sooner or later, however, the young Border Terrier will probably accept the cat as part of its 'pack,' and the two animals may even form a relatively close bond. In the garden, this arrangement can be beneficial to your cat, for the terrier is likely to chase away any other local cats that venture into the area, preventing neighbourhood disputes between rival felines.

As well as cats, Border Terriers will regard rabbits as natural prey. Pet rabbits, therefore, should be kept well away from these terriers. Given the digging ability and determination of this breed of dog, do not rely on a run on the lawn to provide a safe retreat. It is essential that a run housing a rabbit should be wired over the entire base, and not just on the roof and sides, as this will prevent the terrier from gaining access to the run, or squeezing under the side if the ground is uneven. Check, too, that the hutch is secure, with bolts on the door, rather than a simple latch. (The foregoing applies to guinea pigs as well.) In the home, be sure to keep other small pets – such as hamsters – well out of the reach of your Border Terrier. Equally, if you have a pet bird, be sure to exclude the terrier from the room, checking the door is firmly closed before allowing the bird out of its quarters. Other pets, such as tortoises, may also be at risk due to the Border Terrier's strong hunting instincts.

Food and feeding

When you bring your new Border Terrier home, always try to provide the same diet that it was being fed in the kennels or at the breeder's, so that you

A healthy puppy will have a good appetite. Avoid changing its food suddenly, since this can trigger a digestive upset.

minimize the risk of a digestive upset. Any changes to the diet should be made gradually over the course of a week or two, or even up to a month or so, for the same reason.

Just like the original ancestor of all domestic dogs, the Grey Wolf (Canis lupus), the Border Terrier requires an omnivorous diet. All canids are designed to eat predominantly meat-based food, but will eat vegetable matter as well. In fact, there are now special vegetarian dog foods, which are supplemented with all the necessary nutrients required to keep a dog in good health. A dog's metabolism is somewhat different from ours, since it relies mainly on fat and protein as energy sources – and particularly fat. Carbohydrate – in the form of pasta and rice – is of little significance since it is not present in the body of its prey to any major extent, but it is added to commercial dog foods, being a relatively cheap source of nutrients.

It is possible to buy special puppy diets that contain the necessary nutrients to ensure a puppy grows up into a healthy adult dog. All these foods are supplemented with vitamins, which need to be present in the puppy's diet to avoid nutritional deficiencies. Dogs require thirteen different vitamins in their diet which cannot be manufactured in their bodies, although, unlike us, most Border Terriers can produce Vitamin C.

Check which vitamins the dog food contains by looking on the packaging. To retain the potency of the vitamins, make sure you store the food as instructed; you must also use it by the recommended 'use by' date, so that you can be sure your pet will not be affected by a decline in the vitamin content of its food. The effects will vary, depending on which vitamins are missing from the diet. Symptoms associated with deficiencies of so-called water-soluble vitamins, such as members of the Vitamin B complex, usually appear first because these are not stored in the liver, in contrast to the fat-soluble ones, such as Vitamins A, D and E.

Minerals are also a very important component in the diet of Border Terriers and other dogs, and particularly puppies. Calcium is especially vital, with its uptake and regulation in the body under the control of Vitamin D. Another mineral, phosphorus, also plays a vital role in metabolism. The correct calcium:phosphorus ratio should be about 1.2:1, being slanted in favour of calcium, which is a key component of the skeletal system. A deficiency of calcium, a serious imbalance in the calcium:phosphorus ratio (with a higher phosphorus component in the diet), or indeed a deficiency of Vitamin D, are likely to lead to the condition known as rickets.

The inter-relationships between vitamins and minerals, as well as the varying levels which are required in the diet, gives some indication of the difficulty of formulating foods in the correct proportions at home for your Border Terrier. An imbalance in the calcium:phosphorus ratio is especially likely to arise in domestic dogs, because rather than being fed the whole carcass, they tend to be offered just offal, such as melts or tripe, which are low in calcium. Most of the body's calcium stores, in contrast, are retained in the bones. It is therefore no coincidence that prepared dog foods have become so widely used. Puppy foods are used until the age of six months, and then the dogs are moved on to an adult diet. Most so-called 'senior foods' can be used for dogs from about six years onwards, depending on the nutritional information provided on the packaging.

Types of prepared foods

There are three main types of prepared dog food to choose from today. In the past, canned food was by far the most widespread. This is usually predominantly meat based, and can be fed with a form of dry, biscuit-type 'mixer.' Canned foods have faded in popularity recently, being replaced by lightweight pouches of food that usually contain single meal portions and so do not need to be stored in a refrigerator. These 'wet foods' are usually preferred

Measure out the recommended quantity of food carefully, so that you do not overfeed your puppy.

by most Border Terriers, although the breed is not generally fussy about its diet. Border Terriers will also readily eat dry 'complete food,' which represents a more concentrated ration, and so needs only be offered in relatively small amounts. It is very important, given the nature of this type of food, that fresh drinking water is always available. Never allow dry food to become wet in storage; it will become mouldy and will present a serious threat to the terrier's health. Just as with wet foods, there are various life-stage options available in terms of dry diets, starting with puppy food and progressing to a senior ration. However, consider, from your dog's point of view, whether this type of food will be as appetising and interesting as some others ...

Training at mealtimes

Feeding time is an important opportunity to start training your dog, particularly if it is a puppy. Aim to offer food at the same time each day, and your pet will soon come to recognize when it's mealtime. You can then call your puppy to you, helping it to respond to the sound of its name. Encourage the pup to sit, giving this instruction clearly. It will, of course, take time for the puppy to understand what is expected, so start by applying gentle pressure to the hindquarters, and almost immediately it will adopt the required posture; then place the food bowl on the ground. By repeating this process every time you feed your Border Terrier puppy, it will soon learn to respond to the instruction.

Never tease a puppy by putting its food within reach and then taking it away again if it fails to remain sitting for long. This will not only confuse it, but can also trigger aggressive behaviour if the terrier tries to grab the food.

Bear in mind that after eating, a puppy is likely to want to relieve itself, so this is the time to put the young terrier into the garden. It will be beneficial if you set aside part of the garden that can be used effectively as a canine latrine. Initially, stay outdoors with your puppy, to prevent it wandering off around the garden. Try to encourage the terrier to relieve itself in the spot you want it to; using a particular phrase – such as 'toilet,' or 'hurry up,' which your dog will always associate with this action, may be very helpful. As always, give plenty of praise when it behaves as required. With a dog, praise is always a much more effective reinforcement for training than scolding is.

Choosing a vet

A number of factors will influence your choice of vet, including personal recommendations from friends or family members who have pets themselves. However, if you do not know whom to approach, try the local phone book, or search the internet as a useful starting point. It may be worthwhile contacting

Always encourage
your puppy to
sit calmly before
placing its food
bowl on the floor;
don't let it start
jumping around with
excitement ...

... and it's also a
good idea to ask
your puppy to wait
for a few moments
before beginning its
meal.

Although not always the case, dogs tend not to chew their food, but simply bolt it down, provided it can be swallowed easily.

two or three practices to find out how much they charge for vaccinations, and also to establish when they have surgeries. In many cases, though, it may simply be best to pick the practice nearest to you. Then, if you encounter an emergency, help is relatively close at hand. Arrange to take your puppy to the

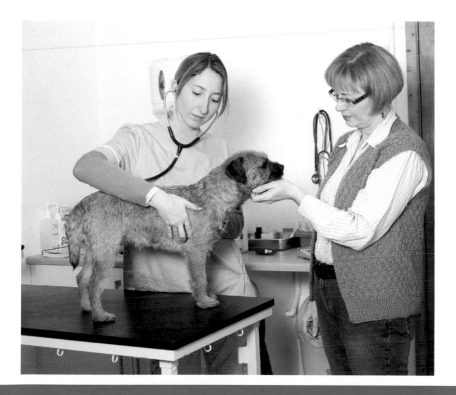

A number of factors will influence which veterinary practice you choose for your Border Terrier, but proximity in the event of any emergency is an important consideration.

practice for a general health check as soon as possible. Should anything show up as a possible concern, such as a cardiac problem, you can notify the seller without delay.

Taking a Border Terrier's temperature. This can give a valuable insight to the problem if your puppy appears to be off-colour.

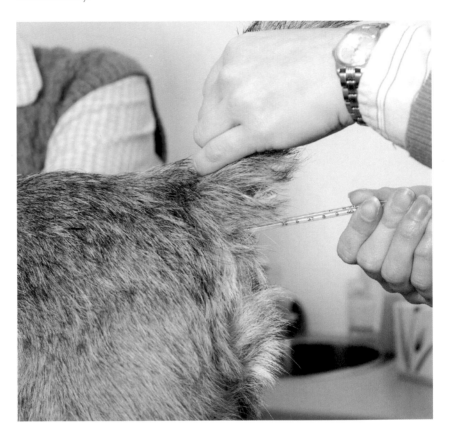

Microchipping

It's important to have your pet microchipped, especially in view of recent legislation, as this provides a lasting means of identity, and is more secure than name tags which can be easily lost. The microchip is implanted under the skin in the neck, in much the same way as a vaccination is given. The chip is about the size of a grain of rice, and contains a unique identification number, which is stored on a central register. Should your puppy stray at any stage in the future, it should be possible to contact you, even if your Border Terrier is no longer wearing its collar and identity tag. All animal welfare bodies involved in dealing with strays have special readers that will activate such chips when passed over the neck area, enabling them to read the code.

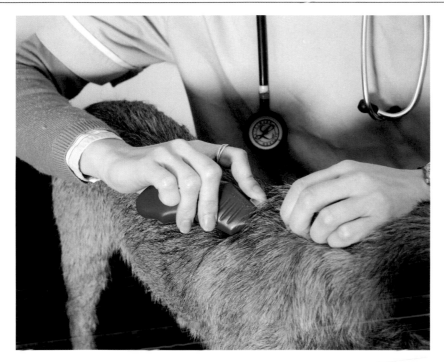

Implanting a microchip. This offers a unique means of identification, allowing your dog to be quickly reunited with you even if the identity disc from its collar is missing.

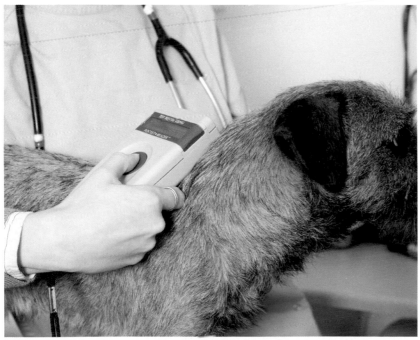

Using a reader to ensure that the newly implanted chip is functioning correctly.

Vaccinations

When you first collected your pet, you should have received a certificate signed and stamped by the vet who gave your puppy its initial set of vaccinations. Take this along to your new vet when you first visit, so that the basic course of vaccinations can be completed. This is usually carried out at twelve weeks of age. About a week or so later it will be safe to allow your puppy out into public places.

Puppies are usually vaccinated against distemper, infectious canine hepatitis, and parvovirus – all of which are serious and potentially fatal viral illnesses affecting dogs – as well as leptospirosis. Protection against leptospirosis is especially important in the case of working Border Terriers, since the bacteria responsible are spread via rat urine. The protection from these vaccines will last for at least a year. Keep your vaccination certificate safe, because you may need to produce it if you put your pet into kennels. There are also other, more specialized vaccines that may be needed, the first of which should give some

Virtually all vaccinations can be given in the scruff of the neck. Like implanting a microchip, this will usually be a relatively painless procedure.

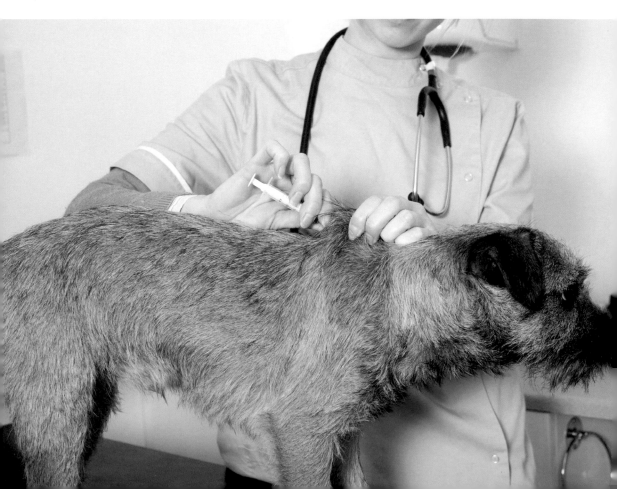

protection against so-called 'kennel cough,' although there is no single cause of this infection and a variety of microbes may be responsible. The vaccine in this case is simply squirted up the dog's nose. Depending partly on where you live – particularly if you are travelling with your dog into mainland Europe from the UK, for example – a rabies vaccination may also be required. Your vet will be able to advise you in this respect.

Deworming

The other treatment that will need to be discussed with your vet at initial consultation is deworming. Puppies can acquire such parasites from their mother, even before birth, and it is very important to dose them with a suitable treatment at regular intervals to eliminate roundworms from their bodies. It is also very important to clear up thoroughly where a puppy has soiled, because worm eggs are expelled in the faeces.

Once in the environment these microscopic eggs can represent a potential hazard, notably to children who may get them on their hands and then ingest them. The eggs can hatch in the intestinal tract and spread around the body via a phase described as 'visceral larval migrans.' If a larva ends up in the eye, it can cause blindness. Always teach children to wash their hands both after touching the dog and then again before meals, to safeguard them against this risk.

Transferring registration documents

Even at an early stage, puppies vary in terms of overall appearance.

Depending on where you acquired your Border Terrier, you may be given its pedigree papers, particularly if you are purchasing a potential show dog: not all Border Terriers are officially registered and sold with pedigrees, however. It will then be up to you to transfer the registration documents into your name, if you wish. This can sometimes be done online – although as far as the Kennel Club in the UK is concerned, this is not always possible. Keep the original paperwork that was given to you by the person who sold you the dog, in case of any query, along with its vaccination certificate. The previous registrant must approve the registration in order for the transfer to proceed; simply registering the Border Terrier in your name is not an indication of legal ownership.

It should be stressed, however, that this very small danger is virtually eliminated by deworming. Working terriers are at greater risk of suffering from both roundworm and tapeworm infections, however, because they can also acquire these parasites from rodents.

As far as roundworms are concerned, you will need to dose your pet every two to three weeks until the age of three months, depending on your vet's advice. For added peace of mind, it is possible to carry out a faecal test to check whether your dog is free of these parasites.

It can be interesting to delve into the records to see which bloodlines your particular Border Terrier is descended from, if you have this information available. The abbreviation 'Ch' in the lineage indicates a breed champion. You will also find that your dog is likely to have a long 'formal' name, under which it is registered. The first part of the name – the so-called 'affix' – indicates the name of the kennels that have contributed to its ancestry. The name you choose for your puppy need bear no relationship to this, but be consistent when you call your dog so that it will readily recognize the sound of its name and come when called. In the case of an older dog, however, it is probably not a good idea to try to change its name, simply because this can be confusing, for obvious reasons.

Visit Hubble and Hattie on the web: www.hubbleandhattie.com and www.hubbleandhattie.blogspot.com
Details of all books • New book news • Special offers

Establishing a daily routine

One of the remarkable features about dogs is the way in which they soon come to regard humans as their 'pack,' adapting quickly to living in a human environment and accepting their place in the scheme of things. Dogs are creatures of habit, who settle well into a daily pattern of life structured around interaction with their owners. To enable them to function properly and to perceive the world around them, dogs rely on a range of different senses, some of which are far more sensitive than ours. Dogs also use a variety of ways to communicate with others of their kind, as well as their human owners. Border Terriers have keen vision and excellent hearing, and their relatively broad nostrils give them a good sense of smell. They can see in colour, although not as acutely as we can, but their night vision is superior to ours, and they are able to see in conditions which would appear as total darkness to our eyes.

The senses and communication

Dogs have a reflective layer on the retina at the back of each eye, known as the tapetum lucidum, which enhances light entering the eyes, making the image

Spend as much time as possible with your new puppy. This will keep the young dog occupied and prevent it from becoming bored and destructive around the home.

Puppies have periods of frenetic activity, and then will quickly fall asleep.

clearer, especially at night. Border Terriers are broad-headed dogs, and, as is usual with predators, the eyes are positioned at the front of their face, rather than at the sides. This gives them a much wider field of view compared with, say, sighthounds (such as Greyhounds), that have narrow faces. It also allows Border Terriers to detect movement over a wide area, and they can easily spot an object such as a rat running for cover, or a toy ball that has been thrown for them. Like many hunting animals, Border Terriers have binocular vision. The overlapping image produced from both eyes enables these terriers to pinpoint the position of prey such as rodents in front of them with great accuracy. So, when they strike, they achieve a high degree of success.

Border Terriers also have much better hearing than humans. While we can detect sounds up to 20,000Hz, Border Terriers may be able to hear frequencies

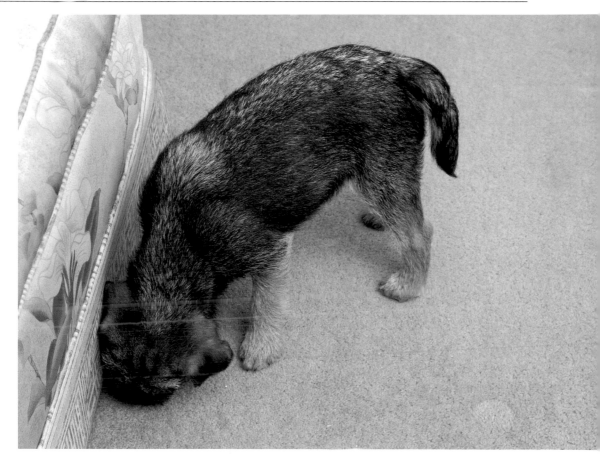

of up to 100,000Hz in the ultrasound band. They fact that they perceive much higher frequencies than humans is evident if you use an ultrasonic dog whistle: the resulting sound will be inaudible to your ears, but can be heard by your dog even if it is some distance away and has disappeared from sight in undergrowth. Nevertheless, just as our hearing range declines with age, so does that of Border Terriers and other dogs. In some cases, dogs may actually become deaf in old age, and their eyesight can fail, too, with whitish cataracts developing in their eyes.

The Border Terrier's olfactory ability will also vary throughout life. Young puppies have a very restricted sense of smell at first, but adult dogs can develop an acute sense of smell which is some 100 times better than our own. This gives them a vital edge when seeking their quarry. If you examine the nostrils of the Border Terrier closely, you will see that these are effectively mobile on

Smell is a vitally important sense for all dogs, and the young Border Terrier will sniff all around its new surroundings.

their outer edges, which enables them to flare. As a consequence, the dog can improve the volume of air that it inhales, triggering specialist cells lining the nasal cavity.

Dogs communicate with each other, and also with humans, in a variety of ways. The most obvious forms of communication are the vocal ones – barking and other noises emitted from the mouth – and the highly visual use of the tail. A dog will vary the tone of its barking to express different moods and meanings. A deeper, determined bark indicates a more aggressive intent than a frequent, short bark, which can mean either frustration or excitement. Tail movements are used to indicate many things to other dogs, as well as to humans, which is why tail docking can have quite adverse effects. Dogs also communicate in lots of other ways, from scent marking to using various types of body language. When you are training your Border Terrier, it is important to be aware of the signs of body language. An excited and enthusiastic dog will raise its tail and lift the position of its ears, which gives its face an alert expression. If nervous or scolded, however, a Border Terrier will lower its tail and flatten the ears against the head

The learning process

Although the Border Terrier has instincts honed over generations, particularly those related to hunting and digging, it is also a breed that is very responsive to training. A puppy is especially likely to make a good pupil, simply because, at this relatively young age, it will be more receptive than an older dog as it learns about the world. There are certain things to bear in mind when training a Border Terrier, however, not least of which is that these dogs have a capacity for independent thought! This is probably another reflection of their ancestry, since these terriers frequently needed to act spontaneously when working.

Some puppies will learn to respond to commands more readily than other individuals. This is quite normal, although there are certain steps you can take to help the training process. To begin with, choose a locality where your puppy can concentrate without any distractions. Another important factor is to keep the training sessions short. Puppies learn by repetition, and so repeating the same thing frequently in several sessions every day will be much more effective than having a marathon session once a week. A young puppy will soon lose interest under these circumstances. Even if your puppy does not always respond as required, be patient: positive reinforcement using encouragement, rewards and praise is by far the most effective way of teaching a puppy. If you do this consistently, your pup will soon understand what is expected of it. The Border Terrier usually responds well to training, to the extent that the breed is often seen in obedience and agility competitions, both of which require close understanding and communication between dog and handler.

House-training

As part of the process of developing into a well-adjusted dog, a young Border Terrier must learn to obey basic commands, and must also be house-trained. Being clean in the house needs to be taught by routine. Observation on your part is also important, and you must be aware of the times when your puppy needs to relieve itself. Puppies have much weaker bladders than adult dogs, and may often urinate up to half a dozen times every day. Once a puppy is asleep, though, its urine production falls naturally, and it can go for longer periods without needing to be placed outdoors to empty its bladder. When a puppy wakes after being asleep, however, it should be placed outdoors immediately, and praised when it does relieve itself, after which it can be allowed back inside again.

Young Border Terriers of both sexes will squat to urinate at first. It is a sign of sexual maturity when male dogs start to cock their leg. Some female dogs may also do this.

It will take from approximately three to six months before the puppy learns to ask to go outdoors of its own accord. When you need to leave your puppy, therefore, keep a low-sided dirt box in its crate, or line the floor of the crate with a thicker than usual layer of newspaper. A good stack of newspapers are necessary at this stage, and you can also buy training pads, which help as well.

When an accident does occur, it is important to clear it up thoroughly otherwise the puppy will be attracted back to the same spot again by the lingering scent, even if the smell is unnoticeable to you. You can buy special preparations that act as a deterrent to this in pet stores. Beware of using an ordinary household disinfectant, especially any pine-based product, since some of these will reinforce the scent, rather than remove it. On the other hand, you can obtain other scent-based products that encourage a puppy to use an area outdoors — although bear in mind these will be washed away by the rain and will have to be reapplied regularly. Do not scold your puppy if it soils in an inappropriate area; the responsibility at this early stage is on you to be there and put the young terrier outdoors on a regular basis. A puppy rapidly learns what is expected of it in terms of house-training, which is not so surprising, given that dogs are naturally clean and much prefer not to soil their immediate environment.

An adult Border Terrier should pose less of a problem, because your new pet is probably used to asking to go out. Even so, you must be alert to its needs at first, in order to develop a routine. Do not be surprised, especially if you are out on a walk, to find that a male dog urinates more frequently than a bitch. This is quite normal, since urine serves as a means of scent marking, and doesn't indicate a weak bladder. Young male Border Terriers are unlikely to raise their hind leg to urinate until they are about six months old, though, because this is a sign of sexual maturity. Until this stage, they will squat like a bitch when they urinate.

Obedience training

Obedience training means teaching your dog to respond to basic commands, such as sitting when told to do so, and coming promptly when called, for example. An obedient dog obviously makes your life easier, and the dog will also benefit by knowing what is expected of it. An obedient dog can also be kept out of danger more easily. A well-trained, dependable Border Terrier is a great source of pleasure, but an individual that is out of control can be a headache for everyone, both in and outside the home. Training learned for a particular purpose can often then be used in other situations; for example, if you train your new puppy to sit when you offer food, you can also use this instruction as a way of preventing the young terrier from jumping around in excitement when you put its lead on before going out for a walk.

Walking on the lead

Once your puppy has completed its course of vaccinations (which usually takes about a month), you can begin basic lead training. The first thing to do is fit the terrier's collar, but don't be surprised if your pet starts to roll around afterwards in an attempt to remove it. This is quite normal, but try to distract it by playing a game instead. A day or so later, attach the lead to the collar. Most terriers will then roll around on the ground once more, and attempt to chew their way through the lead. Again, try to distract your dog from doing this. It is unlikely that your puppy will understand what is required of it when first put on the lead, but, with lots of encouragement, should be up on its feet ready to walk before too long. The initial reaction of the young terrier will be to pull away in all directions, straining on the lead, whereas the aim is to encourage it to walk alongside you.

One of the easiest ways to accomplish this objective is to walk along the side of a fence with your dog; this will act as a barrier and help it to walk in a straight line. Hold the lead in your right hand, with the terrier walking on your left-hand side. Only do this for short periods – perhaps five minutes at a time. When the puppy starts to pull ahead, say 'Stay,' at the same time preventing it from pulling forward. Once the puppy has stopped, press gently on its hindquarters, while saying 'Sit.' Again, it will take time for your new pet to appreciate what is required, so praise the dog lavishly when it responds as required.

'Come'

It is also important to teach your puppy to come to you when called. This training can begin at mealtimes, as mentioned previously, but do this outside, too, and praise your pet when it responds. People often underestimate the value of a puppy mastering this instruction, but under certain circumstances this could save your pet's life if it responds without delay. Unfortunately, this is not always an easy command for Border Terrier puppies to master, as they are somewhat free-spirited, but do persevere, because this is vital. If you acquire an extendible lead (see page 78) play this out, with your puppy sitting while you slowly back away, before calling the dog to you.

Ultimately, you will reach the stage where you can allow your puppy off the lead, at which point you should run through the instructions again. Do not be surprised if your pet's attention wanders somewhat, and with the distractions of unfamiliar scents and surroundings it is unlikely to respond as well as in the relatively quiet and familiar surroundings of your garden. It is a question of being patient, and simply repeating the training exercises that you have been working on together.

At first, walking on a lead will be a strange experience for a young puppy. Be prepared for it to walk across in front of you, and be careful you don't trip over.

Always train a young Border Terrier to sit at the kerb, instead of letting it try to pull ahead, which could be dangerous. Gentle pressure on the hindquarters (above), coupled with the instruction 'sit,' should soon evoke the desired response (below). Always remember to entusiastically praise your puppy when it does as you ask.

Above left: A 'Kong' can very quickly bcome a firm favourite, if stuffed with something good for the puppy to lick out — such as peanut butter. Young Border Terriers need objects like this sterilized bone (above right) that they can chew to ease the pain of teething.

Toys and treats

Successful training depends in part on building a bond between you and your pet, and play presents an important opportunity to create this bond. It also means that you will be able to teach your terrier another important lesson — a willingness to drop items when instructed to do so. Border Terriers have very strong jaws, so it is vital that toys provided for them are suitably robust. Toys that can be destroyed easily pose the risk of parts being swallowed by your dog, which could cause a serious blockage in the digestive tract that can only be rectified by surgery. Provide only recognized brands of chew toys for your pet, therefore, and remember that the urge to chew becomes most evident when the young dog is teething, just before six months of age.

Toys that your terrier can chase are also likely to be popular. They can be taught to chase after flying discs, but only use those

Examples of some of the toys available for your puppy. You will soon find that your pet has its own particular favourites, but all must be safe and robust.

Tugging games are always good fun!

produced specially for dogs. Most Border Terriers prefer chasing after balls, however – which are probably more akin to rodents in their minds. They have a very particular way of playing with a ball, not just using their mouths to pick it up, but sometimes also using their feet to steer it along. Make sure you choose a ball that your terrier can comfortably pick up in its mouth.

A wide range of different treats is for available dogs, but do not be fooled into thinking that your puppy will be deprived without being given a regular supply. There is no need to use treats at all, and, indeed, if you rely on them too much for training purposes, a young dog will soon starting focusing on being given a treat, rather than concentrating on the instruction. Treats can be used to maintain a dog's interest, though, and can be valuable in persuading your terrier to return to you. They can also be combined with so-called 'clicker training' – a method that involves the use of a device that makes a clicking sound, indicating to the dog that it has behaved as required. There is certainly no need to offer packaged treats. Pieces of sliced carrot are a better alternative, since they will not add significantly to the terrier's calorie intake. Prepared beforehand, they can be carried easily in your pocket in a plastic bag. As a naturally active breed, Border Terriers can be at risk of suffering from obesity and its complications if they are overfed, with treats adding unnecessarily to their calorie intake, especially if they do not have sufficient exercise.

Keeping your pet at the correct weight is vital to lessen the risk of health problems, especially as your Border Terrier grows older.

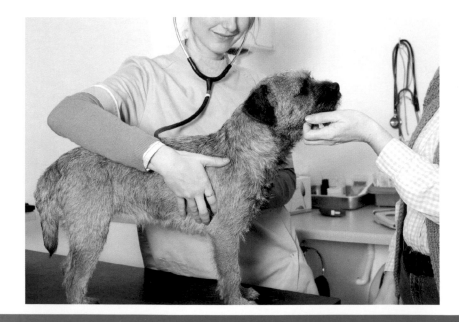

Training classes

If you feel daunted by the prospect of having to train a puppy, you can get guidance by joining a local dog training course. These also have the advantage of allowing your dog to meet other dogs, helping its social development. You can often find such courses by looking in the phone book or local newspapers, on-line, or even via your local library. Alternatively, if you are seeking personal recommendations, ask around your circle of dog-owning friends for good contacts locally. Your veterinary practice may also be able to advise you in this regard.

It's important that you allow your Border Terrier to meet other dogs once it is able to go outside in public spaces.

Weight-watching

It is important to keep a check on your dog's condition to ensure that it is not becoming overweight. This is relatively unlikely in puppies since they are so active, but one of the side-effects of neutering is likely to be a gain in weight through natural metabolic changes. If this happens, you should cut back on the amount of food that your Border Terrier is given. Obesity can dramatically shorten a dog's life, resulting in heart problems and diabetes mellitus. And, just as in humans, too much weight can strain weight-bearing joints such as the hips.

If you acquire an overweight Border Terrier, check with your vet that there is no underlying medical condition that could be the cause of the problem. The practice will be able to work out an individual diet plan for your pet, which you must follow. This is likely to entail a reduction in the amount of food you provide, and possibly also switching to an 'obesity diet' which has a relatively low nutrient, high-fibre content. More exercise will also be important, to burn off the excess calories.

Grooming

Grooming for show purposes requires a considerable degree of skill, although general care of the coat is much more straightforward. The dog's coat consists of two layers: a short, dense undercoat, which provides insulation and helps to protect against injury, and a wiry-textured topcoat.

The undercoat must be stripped twice a year, which keeps it in trim by removing the dead hairs. Stripping can be carried out either by hand or with a stripping knife. If you are particularly keen to learn this skill, there are grooming courses available that will teach you to do this, although many owners keeping

Your Border Terrier is more likely to put on weight after neutering. Regular weighing will be important to detect this at an early stage.

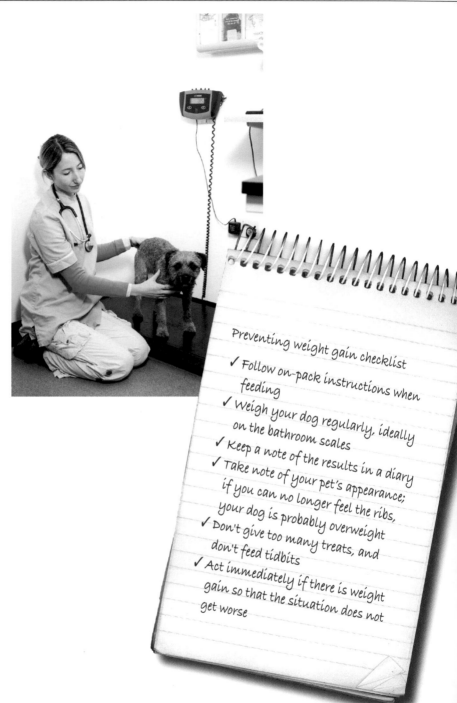

Preventing weight gain checklist

✓ Follow on-pack instructions when feeding

✓ Weigh your dog regularly, ideally on the bathroom scales

✓ Keep a note of the results in a diary

✓ Take note of your pet's appearance; if you can no longer feel the ribs, your dog is probably overweight

✓ Don't give too many treats, and don't feed tidbits

✓ Act immediately if there is weight gain so that the situation does not get worse

Border Terriers solely as pets rely on the services of a local grooming parlour to maintain their dog's coat in top condition. Should you not wish to pay for the cost of hand stripping, then the coat of a pet Border Terrier can be maintained in good condition by clipping, about every three months, although this makes it softer. Otherwise, in terms of general coat care, only a weekly brushing is usually necessary.

As well as offering a chance to assess your dog's condition, grooming – or even simply stroking your pet – provides the opportunity to spot any unexplained lumps on its body that will need veterinary investigation. It also enables you to look for skin parasites such as fleas and ticks.

Specialist grooming equipment for a Border Terrier, plus a safe pair of guillotine-style nail clippers (far right, main photo).

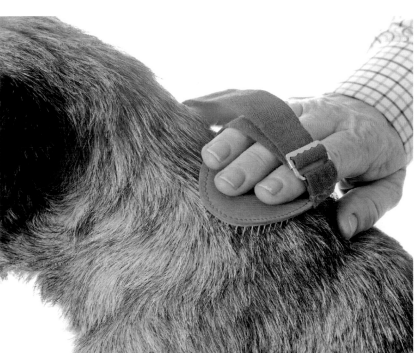

The coat of the Border Terrier has a harsh texture, and is also thick, with the undercoat lying close to the skin.

Grooming not only serves to keep your terrier's coat in good condition, but can also show up parasites. Always check for signs of fleas after grooming. Grooming your dog regularly also helps establish an affinity between you.

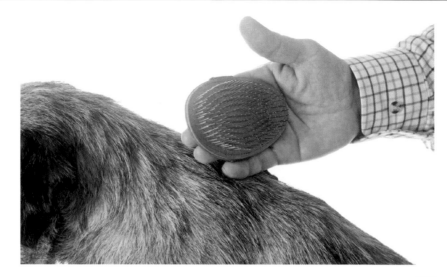

Acclimatise your Border Terrier to being groomed from an early age, so that it will sit still, and grooming will be an easy and pleasurable experience for you both.

Fleas, ticks and mites

All dogs are likely to pick up fleas at some stage. You are less likely to see the fleas than their dirt, however, which will appear as dark specks in the coat. If you are not sure whether these specks indicate the presence of fleas, transfer some of them to a piece of paper and add a drop of water. If they break down, leaving a reddish hue, this confirms it is flea dirt (the colour is produced by the undigested remains of blood on which these parasites feed). As the flea pierces the dog's skin with its mouthparts, it injects saliva into the body. This is likely to provide an even more obvious indication of the presence of fleas, due to persistent scratching by the terrier as it tries to relieve the resulting irritation. A fine-toothed flea comb, used especially in the area of the hindquarters, should locate the fleas. However, they can move very quickly through the coat, thanks partly to their flattened body shape. When you catch them, drop them into some water to prevent them escaping. Grooming the dog outside is also recommended, so if any fleas jump off, they should not pose a problem in the future.

There are products that can be applied directly to a dog's skin to disrupt a flea's breeding cycle, although they will not actually kill adult fleas already present. Always read the instructions carefully before use.

Flea treatment falls into different categories. If you actually find evidence of fleas on your pet, then a flea-killing product must be used. On the other hand, there are now products you can apply in droplet form to the skin of the dog's neck, having parted the fur carefully here beforehand. Flea preparations of this type contain an IGR (insect growth regulator) that the adult flea sucks up from the dog's blood when it feeds. This blocks the development of the immature fleas, preventing any risk of an epidemic in your home. Cats can also spread dog fleas, but note that cats need different flea treatments to dogs. Avoid treating your dog near a pond or an indoor aquarium, since these medications are likely to be fatal to fish.

You may also occasionally find ticks that your terrier has acquired when out walking – usually in rural areas where sheep and cattle are kept, or where deer populations are high. These parasites have a complex lifecycle, and will not breed on the dog, but do present a potentially serious danger since they can transmit a range of blood-borne illnesses, including Lyme's Disease. The tick climbs up on to the dog's body from the undergrowth, and anchors itself in place with its strong mouthparts before starting to feed, swelling significantly as a result. Do not attempt to pull a tick off a dog's body, since this is likely to leave the mouthparts embedded in the skin. Instead, smear the tick's body with petroleum jelly (as sold in a pharmacy), to block its breathing pores, which should cause it to drop off quite rapidly, or use a special tick hook that can be purchased from your vet.

If your Border Terrier persistently scratches at its ears, the cause could be either an infection or an infestation of ear mites.

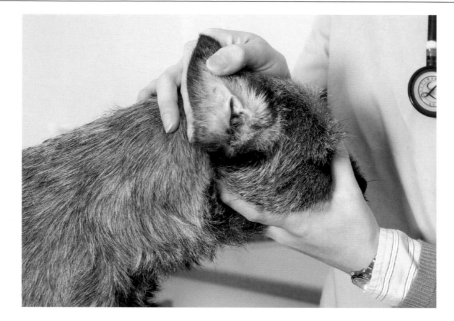

In late summer, if your terrier is out walking with you, it may suddenly start to nibble intently at its feet, and suffering severe irritation there. This is almost certainly caused by an infestation of harvest mite larvae. Be careful if you try to investigate, because your dog will be in severe pain. Immersing the dog's feet in salt water can bring some relief, but an insecticidal shampoo is the best way to eliminate these pests.

Eyes and ears

It can sometimes be necessary to wipe the corner of the eyes carefully with damp cotton wool to remove any tear staining. The external part of the ear canal may benefit from being cleaned gently with a Q-tip, to remove any obvious build-up of dirt and wax, although avoid probing into the ear canal itself, since this could hurt your pet. It could also push debris down into the canal, rather than removing it.

If you notice that your Border Terrier starts scratching its ears, it may have an infection here, and you should seek veterinary advice. Early treatment is vital, because ear problems frequently have a habit of reoccurring. A combination of fungi and bacteria may be the cause, along with ear mites, so a broad-spectrum treatment might be needed. Alternatively, a grass seed may have entered the ear and caused the dog to start scratching, and this will need to be removed by your vet.

Guillotine-type clippers allow the claws to be cut safely. However, it is harder to see the blood supply in black claws, and if the claw is cut too short it will bleed and be very painful for your dog.

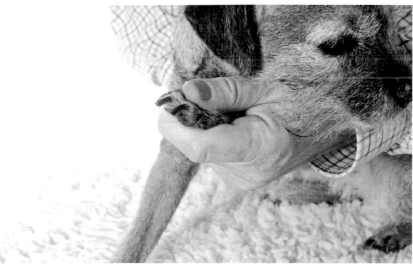

Err on the side of caution when clipping the claws, therefore try to exercise your dog on pavements, gravel paths, and other hard surfaces for some of the time, which will help wear down the claws naturally.

Claws

From an early age get your puppy used to having its feet and toes gently handled. The claws of puppies in particular can be quite sharp, and may benefit from being trimmed back. Again, this is something that you can learn to do yourself, although you should get someone, such as your vet, to show you how to do it correctly. You may also need someone to hold the puppy for you while you cut the claws. The particular difficulty with Border Terriers is that their claws are black, which makes it very hard to locate the blood supply (usually visible as a pinkish streak in a light-coloured claw).

The claws should be cut with a pair of guillotine clippers, which have a sliding blade and a protective edge. Using these should make it easier to avoid cutting the quick, which is the inner part of the claw. If you should cut the quick, however, not only will this be painful for your dog, but it will also cause the claw to start bleeding. Always have a shaving stick available to stem any blood flow in case you accidentally cut the nail too short. Never use scissors to cut a Border Terrier's claws, because these are unlikely to be strong enough to make a clean cut.

Teeth

Dental care is often overlooked, but with terriers and other dogs living longer than ever before, this is now increasingly important – although they can still eat soft food in the absence of most of their teeth. Once again, it is a matter of training a young dog to accept this inspection. First and foremost, you need to be able to open your pet's mouth, so begin by placing your left hand across the upper jaw (assuming you are right-handed), and then you can gently prise down the lower jaw with your other hand. There are both special toothbrushes and toothpaste available now for dogs. Canine toothpaste does not foam up in the mouth like human toothpaste, because dogs would find this distressing. Gently brush the teeth along each jaw line. Once again, puppies can be rather uncooperative, so it will be useful to have someone hold your pet while you do this initially, until it becomes accustomed to the experience. If this still proves too difficult to achieve, you can get a special toothbrush-like attachment that slips over the end of your finger. Try to avoid the dog closing its jaws over your finger as you use this, however, since this will be painful.

A clean, healthy canine tooth, showing no sign of accumulation of tartar around the base. Brushing your Border Terrier's teeth regularly from an early age will help keep them in good condition.

Growing up

To ensure your young terrier does not develop a nervous and fearful nature, it is important to take it out frequently once the course of vaccinations is completed to give it an opportunity to explore and scent mark its environment, as well as socialize with other dogs.

Remember that as Border Terriers become bigger, they can jump higher as well!

Scent marking —
males and females —
becomes increasingly
important to your
dog as it matures.

Border Terriers will
become bolder and
more adventurous
as they leave
puppyhood behind.

Out and about

To begin with, however, concentrate on getting your dog to walk well on a lead, building on the lessons already taught. Keep the puppy walking on your left-hand side, as described in the previous chapter, so it is as far away from the road as possible. Encourage your pet to walk in a straight line by your side and not out in front of you, as you could trip over it! At intervals, pause and get your puppy to sit; something it should do when you come to a kerb and before crossing the road. Always go through the same process, even if the road is clear, so your terrier learns this routine. This is also another reason why the dog should not walk ahead of you: it could easily be hit by a vehicle if it strays even a short distance out into the road.

Kerb training should continue to be reinforced gently but firmly until it becomes second nature. An identity disc on the collar provides an easy way for you to be reunited with your pet if it strays at any stage.

Some owners like to use extending leads, which can permit a young Border Terrier to wander further afield without actually running free.

Young puppies don't need long walks. An ideal situation is perhaps a road walk of some ten to fifteen minutes in the morning (but which will incorporate somewhere suitable for the terrier to relieve itself), followed by a second walk of similar duration out in a park or in the countryside in the afternoon. When walking along the road, keep your puppy close to you on a lead, but allow the dog some freedom to explore when in the countryside. Until you can allow your young Border Terrier to run free, it is useful to put it on an extendible lead, because this gives the puppy more opportunity to roam. Make sure you do not play out too much of the lead, however, or the puppy is likely to become entangled in it as it runs to and fro.

A particular trait of Border Terrier puppies is their naturally inquisitive nature, and holes in the ground are of particular interest. It can be worrying if your dog suddenly disappears out of sight, so don't allow your puppy off the lead in areas such as woodlands or heaths, where rabbit burrows and foxholes may be prevalent, until it has learnt to return to you when called. Even then, you will still need to be alert and keep a close eye on where your pet is wandering, in case it does disappear.

A helpful assistant!
This Border Terrier
chases after its
owner's hat, which
blew off suddenly in
the wind.

Being well trained,
the dog returns
when called,
complete with hat!

Your Border Terrier will get the chance to socialize with many other dogs if exercised regularly in a park, and may even form a bond with some individuals that it meets regularly.

The larger dog shown here is inviting the Border Terrier to play, as shown by the way it has crouched down on its forelegs, with its bottom in the air, in the traditional 'play bow' posture.

Off the lead

When you first let your puppy off the lead, try to avoid doing so in an area where there is a lot of undergrowth; much better is a stretch of open ground, well away from roads and other dogs, hopefully. Call your puppy as necessary to keep it close to you, keeping its attention by throwing a ball or similar toy for it to chase. This will also mean that your terrier must return to you, reinforcing the training previously carried out in the garden.

It is likely that your pet will stay relatively close to you on its first few walks off the lead, but, before long, Border Terriers typically become more adventurous. Do not lose track of your pet's whereabouts when this happens, and keep a look out for other dogs, particularly other breeds of terrier, which are often not be as well disposed towards one of their own kind as other types of dog. Nevertheless, it is important that puppies socialize with older dogs that they meet when out for a walk. It is usually possible to quickly tell if the other dog is likely to be aggressive towards your pet by its body language. Most dogs are fairly tolerant towards puppies, which they generally regard as non-threatening.

The risk of conflict will be higher if you have an older dog, particularly an un-neutered male that will be less inclined to back down in the face of a challenge. Both dogs will square up to each other, hackles raised on their backs, and growling with increasing intensity, with the aim of intimidating their opponent into backing down. Should this not produce the required result, however, the lips are drawn back progressively to reveal the teeth. Ultimately, one dog will launch itself at the other, snarling loudly. Outbreaks of direct conflict are generally brief, with the loser breaking away and being pursued for

Here, an adult Border Terrier responds playfully to a young puppy in the garden.

A Border Terrier rolls over, in a submissive posture, trying to encourage the other dog to play.

When dogs meet, they initially eye each other (top). They then circle around, sniffing in the vicinity of each other's hindquarters (centre). The black and white dog has broken away from the encounter and may then be pursued for a short distance by the Border Terrier (bottom).

a short distance by its opponent. Serious injury is rare, especially if the weaker individual is not trapped and can escape. Should your terrier become involved in a fight, do not try to separate the combatants with your hands, since you could be badly bitten in the fracas. If necessary, use your lead like a lasso to drag your dog away, cautiously fending off the other dog if necessary.

Neutering

One of the best ways to lessen the risk of your terrier being involved in a serious fight is by neutering, particularly in the case of a male dog. Neutering will also result in a cessation of signs of sexual behaviour, and has another significant advantage in terms of decreasing the likelihood that your pet will stray. Known as castration, this surgery involves the removal of both testes.

The equivalent type of surgery in a bitch is known as spaying, and involves removal of the ovaries and uterus. Spaying will prevent any subsequent periods of 'heat' that will otherwise typically occur every six months, when the bitch is likely to become sexually active. Male dogs will almost inevitably pursue her at this stage, as she releases chemical messengers – called pheromones – that are wafted in the air. Even in very minute concentrations, these are still strong enough to attract potential mates from a wide area. Also, by removing the uterus, there is no risk that the bitch may succumb to an infection of the womb called pyometra. This is one of the major illnesses affecting the female's reproductive tract. Spaying also eliminates false pregnancies, which can even result in the production of milk about nine weeks after the last period of heat, around the time when puppies would normally be born.

If your bitch is not neutered, you should not take her out for a walk when she is in season, since she will almost certainly end up mating. Dogs will mate indiscriminately, so any intact male dog can sire a litter of puppies.

Hazards outside the home

Other potential dangers exist which you may encounter when walking with your dog; another reason why it is important to have good control over your pet at all times. Be wary when you are walking near water, particularly rivers, in case your puppy decides to jump in and cannot get out again. Ponds and lakes can become particularly dangerous in winter, too, especially if it is icy. A dog's weight may well be sufficient to break the ice on the surface of a lake or pond, even if it seems thick enough at the margins, plunging the animal into the freezing water beneath.

On beaches where dogs are permitted, beware of the risk of your pet slipping into quicksand, or being swept out to sea by a strong current. Cliff

Bodies of water can be a potential hazard to dogs, especially if they are covered in ice, have steep banks, or are fast flowing.

edges can also be dangerous places for dogs. Always err on the side of caution, therefore, and put your dog on a lead if there is a possibility of danger. This certainly applies when you are close to livestock such as horses and also cows. The latter, in particular, are likely to resent the presence of a dog in their midst, particularly if they have calves. Dogs may also chase or even attack sheep, especially lambing ewes, and so must be kept on a lead at all times when in their vicinity.

Luckily in Britain and much of mainland Europe there is only one venomous snake – the Adder – and none at all in Ireland. However, this is by no means the case in other parts of the world, where there are not just venomous snakes but also powerful constrictor snakes that can easily overpower a Border Terrier. In Britain, dogs usually suffer snake bites from spring until autumn, especially in heathland where Adders tend to live. You are unlikely to see the snake, but the curiosity of a young puppy can lead it into danger. Should you find that your pet suddenly becomes weak and has difficulty walking, the likelihood is that it may have been bitten, in which case you should pick it up and seek veterinary help as soon as possible.

Holiday time

Whether you are holidaying at home or abroad, it is important to make any necessary plans for your pet well in advance. If you are travelling abroad it is now sometimes possible to take your dog with you, depending on where you live and where you are going. For example, you can travel from the UK to other parts of Europe with your pet under what is popularly known as the Pet Passport Scheme, although the scheme is officially described as the Pet Travel

Accident procedures

If your pet has the misfortune to become involved in a road accident, you should again seek veterinary help, even if the animal appears to be relatively unaffected by the event, as there is a possibility of haemorrhage or other internal injury, the effect of which will only become apparent later, by which time it will be much harder to treat successfully. If a dog is left lying in the road after a collision, concentrate first on getting it to safety, rather than trying to assess its injuries while it is still in danger.

Even a normally placid Border Terrier may become aggressive if it is frightened, in pain or in shock, however, and needs to be handled carefully under these circumstances. If possible, use an old blanket or something similar – even a coat – as a makeshift stretcher, and try to keep the dog's body in a relatively horizontal position. This is important because if the diaphragm, which partitions the chest and abdomen, is torn in any way, the organs in the body cavity may become seriously misplaced if the dog is held in an upright position.

Remember that being in pain is likely to affect a Border Terrier's behaviour.

Scheme. Full details of the requirements (which can change from time to time) are to be found on the DEFRA website (see page 85).

Basically, your dog must be vaccinated against the killer disease rabies, in addition to being microchipped, and will also need to be treated against parasites before returning to the UK. You also need to be certain that the journey itself will not be upsetting for your terrier, and that the whole experience will be better than leaving your pet at home. It is perhaps worth remembering that there is a slightly increased risk of your dog succumbing to other 'exotic' diseases – such as leishmaniasis and heartworm – that cannot be guarded against by vaccination, and yet thrive in warmer areas outside Britain.

If you decide not to take your pet, various other options exist. One possibility is to book a home-sitting service to look after your pet in your home. Most home-sitters are retired people who have expertise in looking after animals, but always take up the references of the company concerned before confirming a booking. It is also advisable to contact your insurer to check that you will not be invalidating your cover. Using this type of service also means that your home will not be left empty while you are away. It is likely to be a cost-effective (and convenient) choice if you have a menagerie of creatures, which would otherwise need to be boarded out in your absence.

Kennels

It is important to book boarding kennels as early as possible for your pet, otherwise you might find that there are no vacancies, especially at peak holiday times. People often prefer to use kennels that have been recommended by someone, so ask around among your dog-owning friends before opting for a particular establishment. Alternatively, you can telephone one or two kennels near you, and make an appointment to visit them to satisfy yourself about the care and facilities on offer. Once you have made your choice, you can confirm your booking.

Before taking your Border Terrier to boarding kennels, check that its vaccinations are up to date. You may also need to have your pet treated against kennel cough. Although not generally a serious illness, this can spread rapidly in boarding kennels, and, for this reason, many kennels insist on dogs being vaccinated against the ailment, although this does not protect against every cause of this illness.

Although your dog may seem rather forlorn when you leave, it will almost certainly settle down very quickly in your absence, and you will also have an enthusiastic greeting to look forward to when you return! If you are particularly worried about leaving your terrier, you can book your pet in for a short period, perhaps over a weekend, which should help you decide that all would be well over a longer timespan.

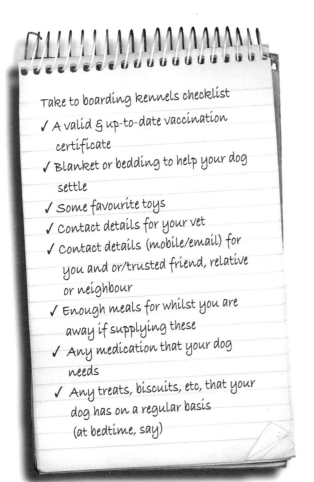

Take to boarding kennels checklist
✓ A valid & up-to-date vaccination certificate
✓ Blanket or bedding to help your dog settle
✓ Some favourite toys
✓ Contact details for your vet
✓ Contact details (mobile/email) for you and or/trusted friend, relative or neighbour
✓ Enough meals for whilst you are away if supplying these
✓ Any medication that your dog needs
✓ Any treats, biscuits, etc, that your dog has on a regular basis (at bedtime, say)

Holidaying with your dog at home

It is, of course, easier to take your dog on holiday with you if you don't go abroad.

There are plenty of good, dog-friendly hotels to be found, with special guidebooks available that list establishments of this type. A long, hot journey by car will be as uncomfortable for your dog as it is for you, so try to make the experience as pleasant as possible by providing plenty of shade and ventilation while travelling. Don't forget to provide ample water as well as some food, and make regular stops so that your dog can stretch its legs and relieve itself if necessary. Remember that it is not safe to leave your dog in a car on its own in the summer, even for a few minutes, because the temperature can rise very rapidly to a fatal level. This may restrict your holiday plans somewhat, especially since many places that you may want to visit, quite apart from restaurants, are also often out of bounds to dogs.

If you are planning a walking holiday, bear in mind that your dog may not be fit enough to cover large distances every day, although Border Terriers do have great stamina. It is something that you may need to build up to, in terms of training, rather than simply embarking on a trek of this type with your dog. In any case, a dog known to be suffering from joint ailments, such as hip dysplasia, should not be subjected to such trips. If you are concerned about your dog's fitness for such a holiday, discuss the idea with your vet before finalizing your plans.

Canal and riverboat holidays can be an excellent option, however, and many boat hire companies allow pets. Your terrier can trot along the towpath at times, and can also sleep on board. Make sure you have a lifejacket for your dog, and maintain a close watch on its whereabouts at all times, keeping it safely on board and under control whenever you are going through locks, or are near deep or fast-flowing water.

Introducing a companion

There may come a time when you decide that you want to introduce another dog into your home. Whether or not this is a Border Terrier, the same rules apply. Start by allowing the dogs to meet each other on neutral territory, in a park, for example, to reduce the risk of conflict. You will need a separate set of feeding dishes for your new pet, because mealtimes represent a potential flashpoint when two dogs are together, and, initially at least, they should be fed separately, in different parts of your home, to prevent one stealing the other's food. It is often much easier to introduce a young puppy alongside an older dog, since each has a clearly defined status, with the younger dog adopting a subordinate role. There is no doubt that an introduction of this type can help rejuvenate an older dog, and, whilst never replacing an old companion, can ease the pain of its death when this happens.

In the home, it is often easier to introduce a young dog to an older, established Border Terrier, rather than another dog of similar age.

Old age

The Border Terrier is a breed that tends not to show its age, these dogs remaining active virtually to the end of their lives. Even so, it is well worth ensuring that your pet receives regular, six-monthly check-ups at the vet's, which can help detect any problem, hopefully, in the early stages, and make the condition easier to manage, even if it cannot be cured. Remain alert to any changes in your pet's behaviour that could be indicative of underlying health problems. If, for example, your dog seems to be losing interest in its food and is having difficulty eating, this can be a sign of a possible dental problem.

Some changes, though, such as a tendency to sleep for longer periods, are quite normal at this stage in life. It's also a good idea to take advantage of the availability of senior diets, which are formulated to meet the precise nutritional needs of older dogs. It is particularly important to prevent your dog from becoming overweight as it gets older, because it can be very difficult to slim down a dog at this stage. Joint ailments, manifested by stiffness, will also be exacerbated in the case of an obese dog.

Ultimately, in spite of all the care, there is likely to come a time when your dog's condition deteriorates to the extent that its quality of life is seriously affected, and it is kinder to put it to sleep. Deciding when your beloved Border Terrier needs to be euthanased is often an extremely hard decision to make, but you can rely on the support of your vet for advice at this exceptionally difficult time.

Afterwards, you may feel that you could not have another member of the

The changes accompanying old age may not always be obvious, although perhaps most noticeably an older Border Terrier will be less active.

Today, much more is known about dietary management and general care, which helps ensure that most Border Terriers can live long, healthy lives.

breed, because it can never replace your previous companion. This is quite understandable, but another Border Terrier will not be a replacement for your previous companion. It will be a different dog, with its own personality and endearing quirks — an individual in its own right. Everyone reacts differently in this situation; you may find that your home and life is so empty without a dog that you get another soon afterwards. Alternatively, you may decide to wait several months. But of one thing you can be sure: owning a Border Terrier will enhance your life.

Further resources

Bibliography

About the Border Terrier Collins, Verite R (Kingdom Books, 1997)
Border Terrier Records 1920-1993 Gillott, William M (W M Gillott, 1993)
Working Terriers, Management and Training Hobson, Jeremy
(The Crowood Press, 1987)
Terriers of the World Horner, Tom (Faber & Faber, 1984)
The Border Terrier Jackson, Frank, and Irving, W Ronald (Foyles, 1969)
All About the Border Terrier Jackson, Frank and Jean (Pelham Books, 1989)
Border Terriers: An Owner's Companion Jackson, Frank and Jean
(The Crowood Press, 1997).
Pet Owner's Guide to the Border Terrier Judge, Betty (Ringpress Books, 1999)
Border Terrier (Best of Breed) Judge, Betty
(The Pet Book Publishing Company, 2009)
The Working Terrier Plummer, Brian (Boydell and Brewer, 1978)
Border Terrier Ruggles-Smythe, Penelope (Petlove, 2000)

Major breed registries in Europe, Africa, Asia and Australia

Australian National Kennel Council, PO Box 285, Red Hill South, Victoria 3937,
Australia
www.ankc.aust.com

Fédération Cynologique Internationale, Place Albert Ier, 13 B-6530 Thuin,
Belgium
www.fci.be

Irish Kennel Club, Fottrell House, Harold's Cross Bridge, Dublin 6W,
Republic of Ireland
www.ikc.ie

The Kennel Club, 1-5 Clarges Street, London, W1Y 8AB, England
www.thekennelclub.org.uk

The Kennel Club of India, Old No 89, New No 28, AA-Block, 1st Street, Anna Nagar, Chennai-600040, India
www.dogsindia.com/registered_kennel_clubs_in_india.htm

The Kennel Union of South Africa (formerly The South African Kennel Club), PO Box 2659, Cape Town 8000, South Africa
www.kusa.co.za/home.php

New Zealand Kennel Club, Prosser Street, Private Bag 50903, Porirua 6220, New Zealand
www.nzkc.org.nz

Major breed registries in North America

American Kennel Club, 260 Madison Avenue, New York, NY 10016, USA
www.akc.org

Canadian Kennel Club, 89 Skyway Avenue, Suite 100, Etobicoke, Ontario M9W 6R4, Canada
www.ckc.ca

Continental Kennel Club, PO Box 1628, Walker, LA 70785, USA
ww.continentalkennelclub.com

National Kennel Club, 255 Indian Ridge Road, PO 331, Blaine, Tennessee 37709, USA
www.nationalkennelclub.co

United Kennel Club, 100 East Kilgore Road, Kalamazoo, MI 49002, USA
www.ukcdogs.com

Universal Kennel Club International, PO 574, Nanuet, NY 10954, USA
www.universalkennel.com

World Kennel Club (registered name), PO 60771, Oklahoma City, OK 73146, USA
www.worldkennelclub.com

World Wide Kennel Club, PO Box 62, Mount Vernon, NY 10552, USA
www.worldwidekennel.qpg.com

More great books from Hubble & Hattie!

Share breakfast, dinner or lunch with your canine friend: this book is packed with scrumptious recipes that you and your dog will love! Tried and tested by Rover and his friends, and approved by a vet for nutritional value, the recipes in this full-colour book will transform mealtimes!

Paperback • 20.5x20.5cm • 112 pages • 100 colour illustrations • ISBN: 978-1-845843-13-7 • £9.99

YOU AND YOUR ...

Everything you need to know about choosing, buying and enjoying the dog of your choice, including breed background, settling in your new arrival, establishing a daily routine, and what to expect as your canine companion grows up. 100 illustrations – many specially commissioned – complete the picture.

Paperback • 22x17cm • 96 pages • 100 colour illustrations • ISBN: 978-1-845843-20-5 • £9.99

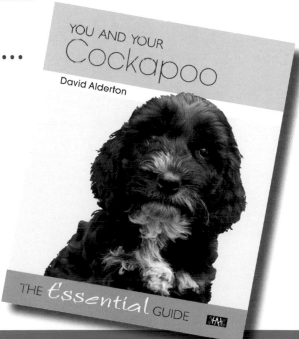

Gentle Dog Care ...

Demonstrates and explains relevant and safe massage for your dog, together with information about how the dog 'works' in relation to what effects massage has.

Paperback • 20.5x20.5cm
• 128 pages • 100 colour illustrations
• ISBN: 978-1-845843-22-9 • £12.99

The technique of this book was developed to ensure that both owner and dog are relaxed, via a combination of breathing and movement exercises for the owner, and stretching, movement and special massage for the dog.
This lovely book holds the secret to a different approach to living and working with your dog.

Paperback • 22x17cm
• 144 pages • 144 colour illustrations
• ISBN: 978-1-845843-33-5 • £14.99

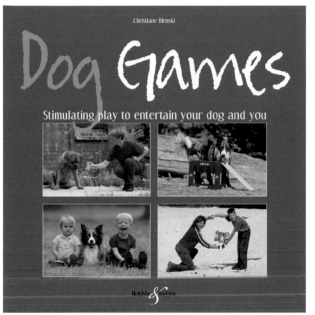

New ideas for games that, after just a quick read of the instructions, allow you and your dog to get on with the fun business of playing. The games in this book will make your dog jump for joy!

Paperback • 25x25cm
• 128 pages • 250
colour illustrations
• ISBN: 978-1-845843-32-8
• £15.95

How does your dog smell? Very well, as it happens! Your faithful friend can be taught to find those lost cars keys, tell you if your food contains minute traces of nuts, or even locate a missing person – and with these nose games, learning how is great fun for you both!

Paperback • 22x17cm
• 80 pages • 38 colour
& 35 b&w illustrations
• ISBN: 978-1-845842-93-2
• £9.99

Index

£9.99 UK • $19.95 USA

STOP!
PLEASE BUY THIS BOOK BEFORE YOU GET ME!

EVERYTHING YOU NEED TO KNOW ABOUT CHOOSING, BUYING, AND ENJOYING YOUR BORDER TERRIER, INCLUDING BREED BACKGROUND, SETTLING IN YOUR NEW ARRIVAL, ESTABLISHING A DAILY ROUTINE, AND WHAT TO EXPECT AS YOUR CANINE COMPANION GROWS UP. SPECIALLY COMMISSIONED PHOTOGRAPHS COLOURFULLY ILLUSTRATE AND DESCRIBE THESE CAPTIVATING LITTLE DOGS

6 36847 04319 3

ISBN 978-1-845843-19-9

9 781845 843199

www.hubbleandhattie.com